Contents

Introduction

Part One VISION
1. Start
2. Define
3. Learn
4. Experiment

Part Two STEER
5. Leap
6. Test
7. Measure
8. Pivot (or Persevere)

Part Three ACCELERATE
9. Batch
10. Grow
11. Adapt
12. Innovate

13. Epilogue: Waste Not

Introduction

Stop me if you've heard this one before. Brilliant college kids sitting in a dorm are inventing the future. Heedless of boundaries, possessed of new technology and youthful enthusiasm, they build a new company from scratch. Their early success allows them to raise money and bring an amazing new product to market. They hire their friends, assemble a superstar team, and dare the world to stop them.

Ten years and several startups ago, that was me, building my first company. I particularly remember a moment from back then: the moment I realized my company was going to fail. My cofounder and I were at our wits' end. The dot-com bubble had burst, and we had spent all our money. We tried desperately to raise more capital, and we could not. It was like a breakup scene from a Hollywood movie: it was raining, and we were arguing in the street. We couldn't even agree on where to walk next, and so we parted in anger, heading in opposite directions. As a metaphor for our company's failure, this image of the two of us, lost in the rain and drifting apart, is perfect.

It remains a painful memory. The company limped along for months afterward, but our situation was hopeless. At the time, it had seemed we were doing everything right: we had a great product, a brilliant team, amazing technology, and the right idea at the right time. And we really were on to something. We were building a way for college kids to create online profiles for the purpose of sharing . . . with employers. Oops. But despite a promising idea, we were nonetheless doomed from day one, because we did not know the process we would need to use to turn our product insights into a great company.

If you've never experienced a failure like this, it is hard to describe the feeling. It's as if the world were falling out from under you. You realize you've been duped. The stories in the magazines are lies: hard work and perseverance don't lead to success. Even worse, the many, many, many promises you've made to employees, friends, and family are not going to come true. Everyone who thought you were foolish for stepping out on your own will be proven right.

It wasn't supposed to turn out that way. In magazines and newspapers, in blockbuster movies, and on countless blogs, we hear the mantra of the successful entrepreneurs: through determination, brilliance, great timing, and—above all—a great product, you too can achieve fame and fortune.

There is a mythmaking industry hard at work to sell us that story, but I have come to believe that the story is false, the product of selection bias and after-the-fact rationalization. In fact, having worked with hundreds of entrepreneurs, I have seen firsthand how often a promising start leads to failure. The grim reality is that most startups fail. Most new products are not successful. Most new ventures do not live up to their potential.

Yet the story of perseverance, creative genius, and hard work persists. Why is it so popular? I think there is something deeply appealing about this modern-day rags-to-riches story. It makes success seem inevitable if you just have the right stuff. It means that the mundane details, the boring stuff, the small individual choices don't matter. If we build it, they will come. When we fail, as so many of us do, we have a ready-made excuse: we didn't have the right stuff. We weren't visionary enough or weren't in the right place at the right time.

After more than ten years as an entrepreneur, I came to reject that line of thinking. I have learned from both my own successes and failures and those of many others that it's the boring stuff that matters the most. Startup success is not a consequence of good genes or being in the right place at the right time. Startup success can be engineered by following the right process, which means it can be learned, which means it can be taught.

Entrepreneurship is a kind of management. No, you didn't read that wrong. We have wildly divergent associations with these two words, *entrepreneurship* and *management*. Lately, it seems that one is cool, innovative, and exciting and the other is dull, serious, and bland. It is time to look past these preconceptions.

Let me tell you a second startup story. It's 2004, and a group of founders have just started a new company. Their previous company had failed very publicly. Their credibility is at an all-time low. They have a huge vision: to change the way people communicate by using a new technology called avatars (remember, this was before James Cameron's blockbuster movie). They are following a visionary named Will Harvey, who paints a compelling picture: people connecting with their friends, hanging out online, using avatars to give them a combination of intimate connection and safe anonymity. Even better, instead of having to build all the clothing, furniture, and accessories these avatars would need to accessorize their digital lives, the customers would be enlisted to build those things and sell them to one another.

The engineering challenge before them is immense: creating virtual worlds, user-generated content, an online commerce engine, micropayments, and—last but not least—the three-dimensional avatar technology that can run on anyone's PC.

I'm in this second story, too. I'm a cofounder and chief technology officer of this company, which is called IMVU. At this point in our careers, my cofounders and I are determined to make new mistakes. We do everything wrong: instead of spending years perfecting our technology, we build a minimum viable product, an early product that is terrible, full of bugs and crash-your-computer-yes-really stability problems. Then we ship it to customers way before it's ready. And we charge money for it. After securing initial customers, we change the product constantly—much too fast by traditional standards—shipping new versions of our product dozens of times every single day.

We really did have customers in those early days—true visionary early adopters—and we often talked to them and asked for their feedback. But we emphatically did *not* do what they said. We viewed their input as only one source of information about our product and overall vision. In fact, we were much more likely to run experiments on our customers than we were to cater to their whims.

Traditional business thinking says that this approach shouldn't work, but it does, and you don't have to take my word for it. As you'll see throughout this book, the approach we pioneered at IMVU has become the basis for a new movement of entrepreneurs around the world. It builds on many previous management and product development ideas, including lean manufacturing, design thinking, customer development, and agile development. It represents a new approach to creating continuous innovation. It's called the Lean Startup.

Despite the volumes written on business strategy, the key attributes of business leaders, and ways to identify the next big thing, innovators still struggle to bring their ideas to life. This was the frustration that led us to try a radical new approach at IMVU, one characterized by an extremely fast cycle time, a focus on what customers want (without asking them), and a scientific approach to making decisions.

ORIGINS OF THE LEAN STARTUP

I am one of those people who grew up programming computers, and so my journey to thinking about entrepreneurship and management has taken a circuitous path. I have always worked on the product development side of my industry; my partners and bosses were managers or marketers, and my peers worked in engineering and operations. Throughout my career, I kept having the experience of working incredibly hard on products that ultimately failed in the marketplace.

At first, largely because of my background, I viewed these as technical problems that required technical solutions: better architecture, a better engineering process, better discipline, focus, or product vision. These supposed fixes led to still more failure. So I read everything I could get my hands on and was blessed to have had some of the top minds in Silicon Valley as my mentors. By the time I became a cofounder of IMVU, I was hungry for new ideas about how to build a company.

I was fortunate to have cofounders who were willing to experiment with new approaches. They were fed up—as I was—by the failure of traditional thinking. Also, we were lucky to have Steve Blank as an investor and adviser. Back in 2004, Steve had just begun preaching a new idea: the business and marketing functions of a startup should be considered as important as engineering and product development and therefore deserve an equally rigorous methodology to guide them. He called that methodology Customer Development, and it offered insight and guidance to my daily work as an entrepreneur.

Meanwhile, I was building IMVU's product development team, using some of the unorthodox methods I mentioned earlier. Measured against the traditional theories of product development I had been trained on in my career, these methods did not make sense, yet I could see firsthand that they were working. I struggled to explain the practices to new employees, investors, and the founders of other companies. We lacked a common language for describing them and concrete principles for understanding them.

I began to search outside entrepreneurship for ideas that could help me make sense of my experience. I began to study other industries, especially manufacturing, from which most modern theories of management derive. I studied lean manufacturing, a process that originated in Japan with the Toyota Production System, a completely new way of thinking about the manufacturing of physical goods. I found that by applying ideas from lean manufacturing to my own entrepreneurial challenges—with a few tweaks and changes—I had the beginnings of a framework for making sense of them.

This line of thought evolved into the Lean Startup: the application of lean thinking to the process of innovation.

IMVU became a tremendous success. IMVU customers have created more than 60 million avatars. It is a profitable company with annual revenues of more than $50 million in 2011, employing more than a hundred people in our current offices in Mountain View, California. IMVU's virtual goods catalog—which seemed so risky years ago—now has more than 6 million items in it; more than 7,000 are added every day, almost all created by customers.

As a result of IMVU's success, I began to be asked for advice by other startups and venture capitalists. When I would describe my experiences at IMVU, I was often met with blank stares or extreme skepticism. The most common reply was "That could never work!" My experience so flew in the face of conventional thinking that most people, even in the innovation hub of Silicon Valley, could not wrap their minds around it.

Then I started to write, first on a blog called *Startup Lessons Learned*, and speak—at conferences and to companies, startups, and venture capitalists—to anyone who would listen. In the process of being called on to defend and explain my insights and with the collaboration of other writers, thinkers, and entrepreneurs, I had a chance to refine and develop the theory of the Lean Startup beyond its rudimentary beginnings. My hope all along was to find ways to eliminate the tremendous waste I saw all around me: startups that built products nobody wanted, new products pulled from the shelves, countless dreams unrealized.

Eventually, the Lean Startup idea blossomed into a global movement. Entrepreneurs began forming local in-person groups to discuss and apply Lean Startup ideas. There are now organized communities of practice in more than a hundred cities around the world.[1] My travels have taken me across countries and continents. Everywhere I have seen the signs of a new entrepreneurial renaissance. The Lean Startup movement is making entrepreneurship accessible to a whole new generation of founders who are hungry for new ideas about how to build successful companies.

Although my background is in high-tech software entrepreneurship, the movement has grown way beyond those roots. Thousands of entrepreneurs are putting Lean Startup principles to work in every conceivable industry. I've had the chance to work with entrepreneurs in companies of all sizes, in different industries, and even in government. This journey has taken me to places I never imagined I'd see, from the world's most elite venture capitalists, to Fortune 500 boardrooms, to the Pentagon. The most nervous I have ever been in a meeting was when

I was attempting to explain Lean Startup principles to the chief information officer of the U.S. Army, who is a three-star general (for the record, he was extremely open to new ideas, even from a civilian like me).

Pretty soon I realized that it was time to focus on the Lean Startup movement full time. My mission: to improve the success rate of new innovative products worldwide. The result is the book you are reading.

THE LEAN STARTUP METHOD

This is a book for entrepreneurs and the people who hold them accountable. The five principles of the Lean Startup, which inform all three parts of this book, are as follows:

1. Entrepreneurs are everywhere. You don't have to work in a garage to be in a startup. The concept of entrepreneurship includes anyone who works within my definition of a startup: a human institution designed to create new products and services under conditions of extreme uncertainty. That means entrepreneurs are everywhere and the Lean Startup approach can work in any size company, even a very large enterprise, in any sector or industry.

2. Entrepreneurship is management. A startup is an institution, not just a product, and so it requires a new kind of management specifically geared to its context of extreme uncertainty. In fact, as I will argue later, I believe "entrepreneur" should be considered a job title in all modern companies that depend on innovation for their future growth.

3. Validated learning. Startups exist not just to make stuff, make money, or even serve customers. They exist to *learn* how to build a sustainable business. This learning can be validated scientifically by running frequent experiments that allow entrepreneurs to test each element of their vision.

4. Build-Measure-Learn. The fundamental activity of a startup is to turn ideas into products, measure how customers respond, and then learn whether to pivot or persevere. All successful startup processes should be geared to accelerate that feedback loop.

5. Innovation accounting. To improve entrepreneurial outcomes and hold innovators accountable, we need to focus on the boring stuff: how to measure progress, how to set up milestones, and how to prioritize work. This requires a new kind of accounting designed for startups—and the people who hold them accountable.

Why Startups Fail

Why are startups failing so badly everywhere we look?

The first problem is the allure of a good plan, a solid strategy, and thorough market research. In earlier eras, these things were indicators of likely success. The overwhelming temptation is to apply them to startups too, but this doesn't work, because startups operate with too much uncertainty. Startups do not yet know who their customer is or what their product should be. As the world becomes more uncertain, it gets harder and harder to predict the future. The old management methods are not up to the task. Planning and forecasting are only accurate when based on a long, stable operating history and a relatively static environment. Startups have neither.

The second problem is that after seeing traditional management fail to solve this problem, some entrepreneurs and investors have thrown up their hands and adopted the "Just Do It" school of startups. This school believes that if management is the problem, chaos is the answer. Unfortunately, as I can attest firsthand, this doesn't work either.

It may seem counterintuitive to think that something as disruptive, innovative, and chaotic as a startup can be managed or, to be accurate, *must* be managed. Most people think of process and management as boring and dull, whereas startups are dynamic and exciting. But what is actually exciting is to see startups succeed and change the world. The passion, energy, and vision that people bring to these new ventures are resources too precious to waste. We can—and must—do better. This book is about how.

HOW THIS BOOK IS ORGANIZED

This book is divided into three parts: "Vision," "Steer," and "Accelerate."

"Vision" makes the case for a new discipline of entrepreneurial management. I identify who is an entrepreneur, define a startup, and articulate a new way for startups to gauge if they are making progress, called validated learning. To achieve that learning, we'll see that startups—in a garage or inside an enterprise—can use scientific experimentation to discover how to build a sustainable business.

"Steer" dives into the Lean Startup method in detail, showing one major turn through the core Build-Measure-Learn feedback loop. Beginning with leap-of-faith assumptions that cry out for rigorous testing, you'll learn how to build a minimum viable product to test those assumptions, a new accounting system for evaluating whether you're making progress, and a method for deciding whether to pivot (changing course with one foot anchored to the ground) or persevere.

In "Accelerate," we'll explore techniques that enable Lean Startups to speed through the Build-Measure-Learn feedback loop as quickly as possible, even as they scale. We'll explore lean manufacturing concepts that are applicable to startups, too, such as the power of small batches. We'll also discuss organizational design, how products grow, and how to apply Lean Startup principles beyond the proverbial garage, even inside the world's largest companies.

MANAGEMENT'S SECOND CENTURY

As a society, we have a proven set of techniques for managing big companies and we know the best practices for building physical products. But when it comes to startups and innovation, we are still shooting in the dark. We are relying on vision, chasing the "great men" who can make magic happen, or trying to analyze our new products to death. These are new problems, born of the success of management in the twentieth century.

This book attempts to put entrepreneurship and innovation on a rigorous footing. We are at the dawn of management's second century. It is our challenge to do something great with the opportunity we have been given. The Lean Startup movement seeks to ensure that those of us who long to build the next big thing will have the tools we need to change the world.

Part One
VISION

1
START

ENTREPRENEURIAL MANAGEMENT

Building a startup is an exercise in institution building; thus, it necessarily involves management. This often comes as a surprise to aspiring entrepreneurs, because their associations with these two words are so diametrically opposed. Entrepreneurs are rightly wary of implementing traditional management practices early on in a startup, afraid that they will invite bureaucracy or stifle creativity.

Entrepreneurs have been trying to fit the square peg of their unique problems into the round hole of general management for decades. As a result, many entrepreneurs take a "just do it" attitude, avoiding all forms of management, process, and discipline. Unfortunately, this approach leads to chaos more often than it does to success. I should know: my first startup failures were all of this kind.

The tremendous success of general management over the last century has provided unprecedented material abundance, but those management principles are ill suited to handle the chaos and uncertainty that startups must face.

o o o

I believe that entrepreneurship requires a managerial discipline to harness the entrepreneurial opportunity we have been given.

There are more entrepreneurs operating today than at any previous time in history. This has been made possible by dramatic changes in the global economy. To cite but one example, one often hears commentators lament the loss of manufacturing jobs in the United States over the previous two decades, but one rarely hears about a corresponding loss of manufacturing capability. That's because total manufacturing output in the United States is *increasing* (by 15 percent in the last decade) even as jobs continue to be lost (see the charts below). In effect, the huge productivity increases made possible by modern management and technology have created more productive capacity than firms know what to do with.[1]

We are living through an unprecedented worldwide entrepreneurial renaissance, but this opportunity is laced with peril.

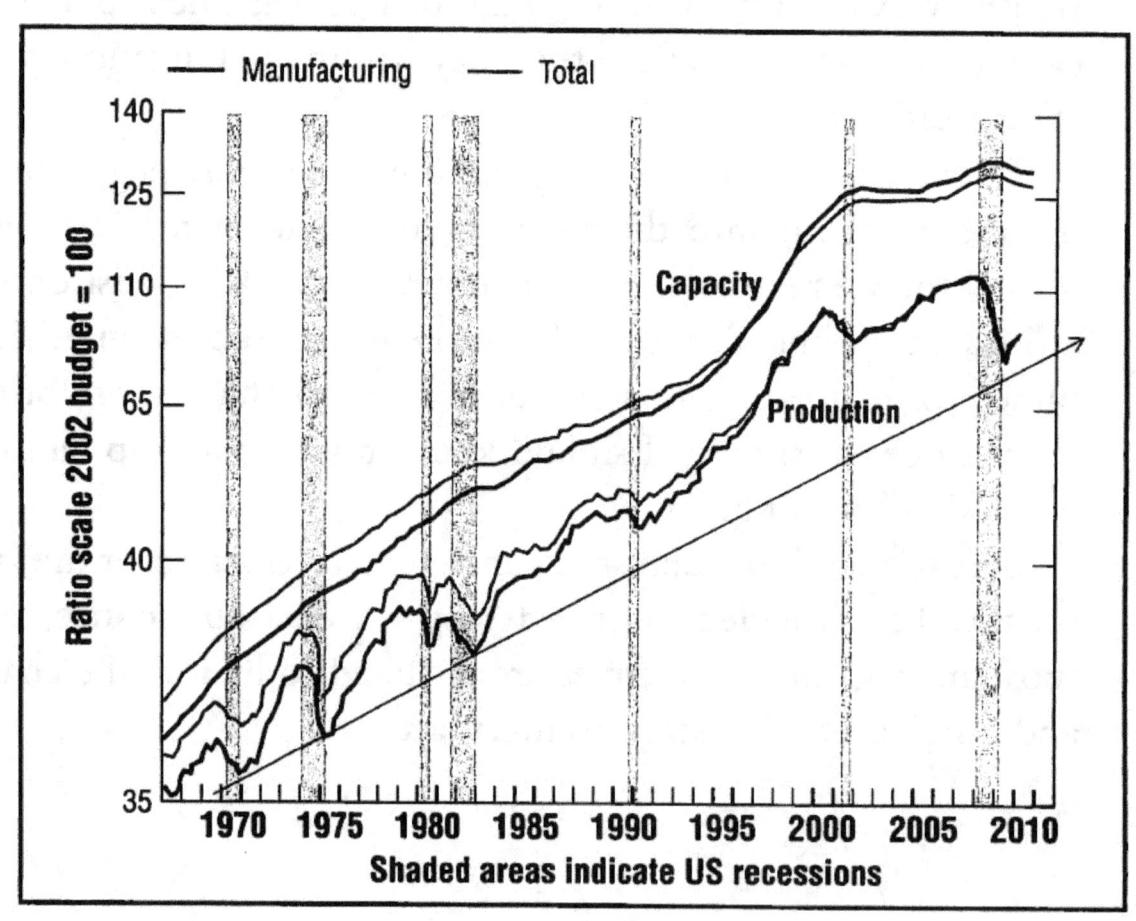

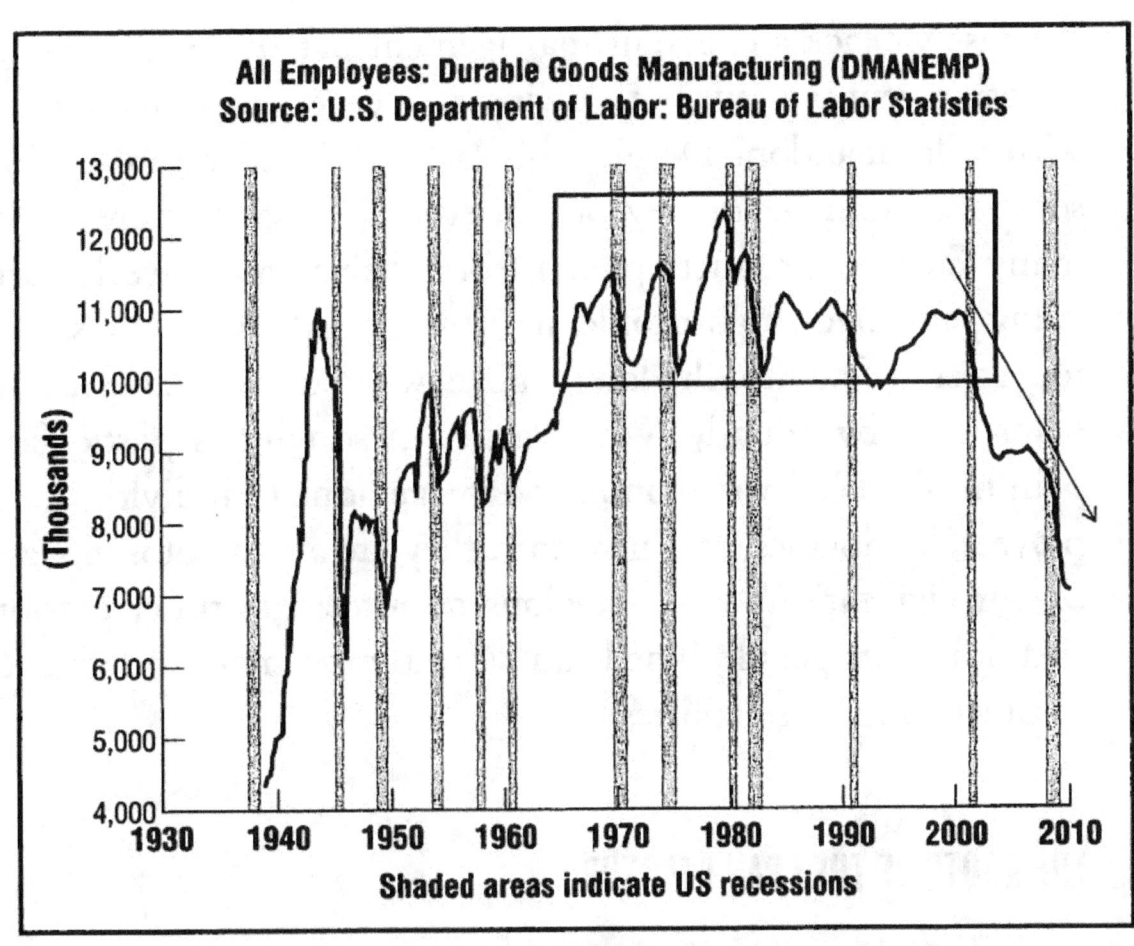
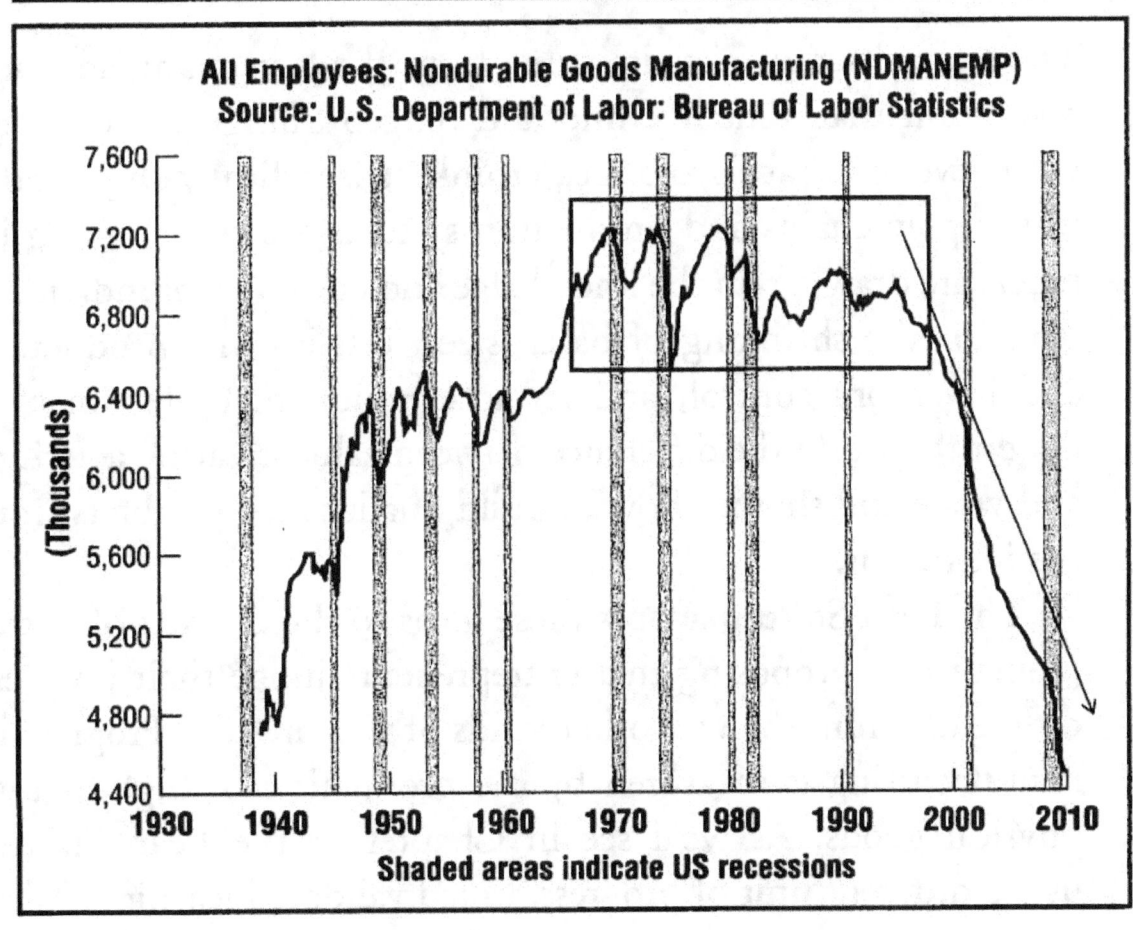

Because we lack a coherent management paradigm for new innovative ventures, we're throwing our excess capacity around with wild abandon. Despite this lack of rigor, we are finding some ways to make money, but for every success there are far too many failures: products pulled from shelves mere weeks after being launched, high-profile startups lauded in the press and forgotten a few months later, and new products that wind up being used by nobody. What makes these failures particularly painful is not just the economic damage done to individual employees, companies, and investors; they are also a colossal waste of our civilization's most precious resource: the time, passion, and skill of its people. The Lean Startup movement is dedicated to preventing these failures.

THE ROOTS OF THE LEAN STARTUP

The Lean Startup takes its name from the lean manufacturing revolution that Taiichi Ohno and Shigeo Shingo are credited with developing at Toyota. Lean thinking is radically altering the way supply chains and production systems are run. Among its tenets are drawing on the knowledge and creativity of individual workers, the shrinking of batch sizes, just-in-time production and inventory control, and an acceleration of cycle times. It taught the world the difference between value-creating activities and waste and showed how to build quality into products from the inside out.

The Lean Startup adapts these ideas to the context of entrepreneurship, proposing that entrepreneurs judge their progress differently from the way other kinds of ventures do. Progress in manufacturing is measured by the production of high-quality physical goods. As we'll see in Chapter 3, the Lean Startup uses a different unit of progress, called validated learning. With scientific learning as our yardstick, we can discover and eliminate the sources of waste that are plaguing entrepreneurship.

A comprehensive theory of entrepreneurship should address all the functions of an early-stage venture: vision and concept, product development, marketing and sales, scaling up, partnerships and distribution, and structure and organizational design. It has to provide a method for measuring progress in the context of extreme uncertainty. It can give entrepreneurs clear guidance on how to make the many trade-off decisions they face: whether and when to invest in process; formulating, planning, and creating infrastructure; when to go it alone and when to partner; when to respond to feedback and when to stick with vision; and how and when to invest in scaling the business. Most of all, it must allow entrepreneurs to make testable predictions.

For example, consider the recommendation that you build cross-functional teams and hold them accountable to what we call *learning milestones* instead of organizing your company into strict functional departments (marketing, sales, information technology, human resources, etc.) that hold people accountable for performing well in their specialized areas (see Chapter 7). Perhaps you agree with this recommendation, or perhaps you are skeptical. Either way, if you decide to implement it, I predict that you pretty quickly will get feedback from your teams that the new process is reducing their productivity. They will ask to go back to the old way of working, in which they had the opportunity to "stay efficient" by working in larger batches and passing work between departments.

It's safe to predict this result, and not just because I have seen it many times in the companies I work with. It is a straightforward prediction of the Lean Startup theory itself. When people are used to evaluating their productivity locally, they feel that a good day is one in which they did their job well all day. When I worked as a programmer, that meant eight straight hours of programming without interruption. That was a good day. In contrast, if I was interrupted with questions, process, or—heaven forbid—meetings, I felt bad. What did I really accomplish that day? Code and product features were tangible to me; I could see them, understand them, and show them off. Learning, by contrast, is frustratingly intangible.

The Lean Startup asks people to start measuring their productivity differently. Because startups often accidentally build something nobody wants, it doesn't matter much if they do it on time and on budget. The goal of a startup is to figure out the right thing to build—the thing customers want and will pay for—as quickly as possible. In other words, the Lean Startup is a new way of looking at the development of innovative new products that emphasizes fast iteration and customer insight, a huge vision, and great ambition, all at the same time.

o o o

Henry Ford is one of the most successful and celebrated entrepreneurs of all time. Since the idea of management has been bound up with the history of the automobile since its first days, I believe it is fitting to use the automobile as a metaphor for a startup.

An internal combustion automobile is powered by two important and very different feedback loops. The first feedback loop is deep inside the engine. Before Henry Ford was a famous CEO, he was an engineer. He spent his days and nights tinkering in his garage with the precise mechanics of getting the engine cylinders to move. Each tiny explosion within the cylinder provides the motive force to turn the wheels but also drives the ignition of the next explosion. Unless the timing of this feedback loop is managed precisely, the engine will sputter and break down.

Startups have a similar engine that I call the *engine of growth*. The markets and customers for startups are diverse: a toy company, a consulting firm, and a manufacturing plant may not seem like they have much in common, but, as we'll see, they operate with the same engine of growth.

Every new version of a product, every new feature, and every new marketing program is an attempt to improve this engine of growth. Like Henry Ford's tinkering in his garage, not all of these changes turn out to be improvements. New product development happens in fits and starts. Much of the time in a startup's life is spent tuning the engine by making improvements in product, marketing, or operations.

The second important feedback loop in an automobile is between the driver and the steering wheel. This feedback is so immediate and automatic that we often don't think about it, but it is steering that differentiates driving from most other forms of transportation. If you have a daily commute, you probably know the route so well that your hands seem to steer you there on their own accord. We can practically drive the route in our sleep. Yet if I asked you to close your eyes and write down exactly how to get to your office—not the street directions but every action you need to take, every push of hand on wheel and foot on pedals—you'd find it impossible. The choreography of driving is incredibly complex when one slows down to think about it.

By contrast, a rocket ship requires just this kind of in-advance calibration. It must be launched with the most precise instructions on what to do: every thrust, every firing of a booster, and every change in direction. The tiniest error at the point of launch could yield catastrophic results thousands of miles later.

Unfortunately, too many startup business plans look more like they are planning to launch a rocket ship than drive a car. They prescribe the steps to take and the results to expect in excruciating detail, and as in planning to launch a rocket, they are set up in such a way that even tiny errors in assumptions can lead to catastrophic outcomes.

One company I worked with had the misfortune of forecasting significant customer adoption—in the millions—for one of its new products. Powered by a splashy launch, the company successfully executed its plan. Unfortunately, customers did not flock to the product in great numbers. Even worse, the company had invested in massive infrastructure, hiring, and support to handle the influx of customers it expected. When the customers failed to materialize, the company had committed itself so completely that they could not adapt in time. They had "achieved failure"—successfully, faithfully, and rigorously executing a plan that turned out to have been utterly flawed.

The Lean Startup method, in contrast, is designed to teach you how to drive a startup. Instead of making complex plans that are based on a lot of assumptions, you can make constant adjustments with a steering wheel called the *Build-Measure-Learn* feedback loop. Through this process of steering, we can learn when and if it's time to make a sharp turn called a *pivot* or whether we should *persevere* along our current path. Once we have an engine that's revved up, the Lean Startup offers methods to scale and grow the business with maximum acceleration.

Throughout the process of driving, you always have a clear idea of where you're going. If you're commuting to work, you don't give up because there's a detour in the road or you made a wrong turn. You remain thoroughly focused on getting to your destination.

Startups also have a true north, a destination in mind: creating a thriving and world-changing business. I call that a startup's *vision*. To achieve that vision, startups employ a *strategy*, which includes a business model, a product road map, a point of view about partners and competitors, and ideas about who the customer will be. The *product* is the end result of this strategy (see the chart on page 23).

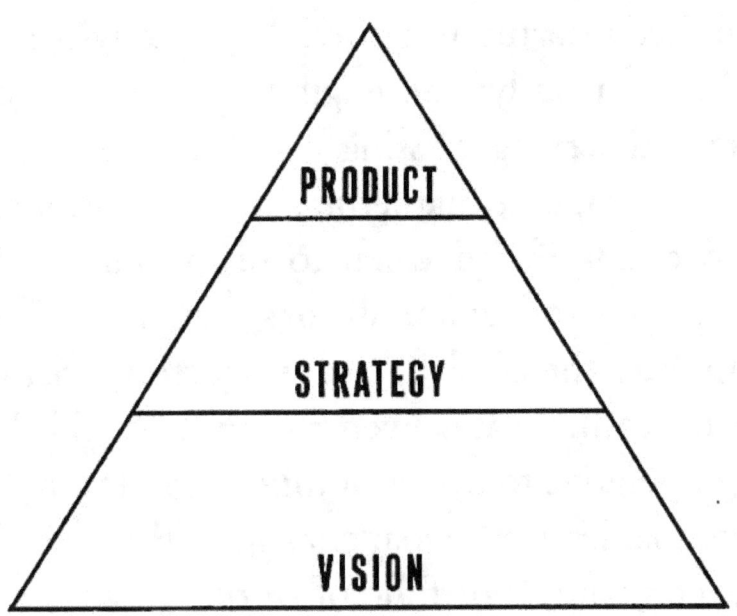

Products change constantly through the process of optimization, what I call *tuning the engine*. Less frequently, the strategy may have to change (called a pivot). However, the overarching vision rarely changes. Entrepreneurs are committed to seeing the startup through to that destination. Every setback is an opportunity for learning how to get where they want to go (see the chart below).

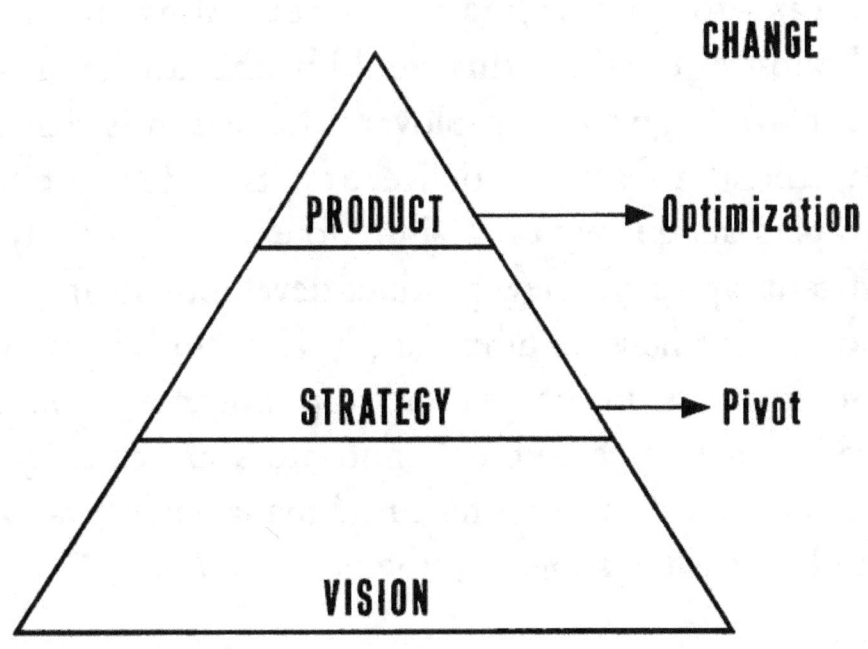

In real life, a startup is a portfolio of activities. A lot is happening simultaneously: the engine is running, acquiring new customers and serving existing ones; we are tuning, trying to improve our product, marketing, and operations; and we are steering, deciding if and when to pivot. The challenge of entrepreneurship is to balance all these activities. Even the smallest startup faces the challenge of supporting existing customers while trying to innovate. Even the most established company faces the imperative to invest in innovation lest it become obsolete. As companies grow, what changes is the mix of these activities in the company's portfolio of work.

o o o

Entrepreneurship is management. And yet, imagine a modern manager who is tasked with building a new product in the context of an established company. Imagine that she goes back to her company's chief financial officer (CFO) a year later and says, "We have failed to meet the growth targets we predicted. In fact, we have almost no new customers and no new revenue. However, we have learned an incredible amount and are on the cusp of a breakthrough new line of business. All we need is another year." Most of the time, this would be the last report this intrapreneur would give her employer. The reason is that in general management, a failure to deliver results is due to either a failure to plan adequately or a failure to execute properly. Both are significant lapses, yet new product development in our modern economy routinely requires exactly this kind of failure on the way to greatness. In the Lean Startup movement, we have come to realize that these internal innovators are actually entrepreneurs, too, and that entrepreneurial management can help them succeed; this is the subject of the next chapter.

2
DEFINE

WHO, EXACTLY, IS AN ENTREPRENEUR?

As I travel the world talking about the Lean Startup, I'm consistently surprised that I meet people in the audience who seem out of place. In addition to the more traditional startup entrepreneurs I meet, these people are general managers, mostly working in very large companies, who are tasked with creating new ventures or product innovations. They are adept at organizational politics: they know how to form autonomous divisions with separate profit and loss statements (P&Ls) and can shield controversial teams from corporate meddling. The biggest surprise is that they are visionaries. Like the startup founders I have worked with for years, they can see the future of their industries and are prepared to take bold risks to seek out new and innovative solutions to the problems their companies face.

Mark, for example, is a manager for an extremely large company who came to one of my lectures. He is the leader of a division that recently had been chartered to bring his company into the twenty-first century by building a new suite of products designed to take advantage of the Internet. When he came to talk to me afterward, I started to give him the standard advice about how to create innovation teams inside big companies, and he stopped me in midstream: "Yeah, I've read *The Innovator's Dilemma*.[1] I've got that all taken care of." He was a long-term employee of the company and a successful manager to boot, so managing internal politics was the least of his problems. I should have known; his success was a testament to his ability to navigate the company's corporate policies, personnel, and processes to get things done.

Next, I tried to give him some advice about the future, about cool new highly leveraged product development technologies. He interrupted me again: "Right. I know all about the Internet, and I have a vision for how our company needs to adapt to it or die."

Mark has all the entrepreneurial *prerequisites* nailed—proper team structure, good personnel, a strong vision for the future, and an appetite for risk taking—and so it finally occurred to me to ask why he was coming to me for advice. He said, "It's as if we have all of the raw materials: kindling, wood, paper, flint, even some sparks. But where's the fire?" The theories of management that Mark had studied treat innovation like a "black box" by focusing on the structures companies need to put in place to form internal startup teams. But Mark found himself working *inside the black box*—and in need of guidance.

What Mark was missing was a process for converting the raw materials of innovation into real-world breakthrough successes. Once a team is set up, what should it do? What process should it use? How should it be held accountable to performance milestones? These are questions the Lean Startup methodology is designed to answer.

My point? Mark is an entrepreneur just like a Silicon Valley high-tech founder with a garage startup. He needs the principles of the Lean Startup just as much as the folks I thought of as classic entrepreneurs do.

Entrepreneurs who operate inside an established organization sometimes are called "intrapreneurs" because of the special circumstances that attend building a startup within a larger company. As I have applied Lean Startup ideas in an ever-widening variety of companies and industries, I have come to believe that intrapreneurs have much more in common with the rest of the community of entrepreneurs than most people believe. Thus, when I use the term *entrepreneur,* I am referring to the whole startup ecosystem regardless of company size, sector, or stage of development.

This book is for entrepreneurs of all stripes: from young visionaries with little backing but great ideas to seasoned visionaries within larger companies such as Mark—and the people who hold them accountable.

IF I'M AN ENTREPRENEUR, WHAT'S A STARTUP?

The Lean Startup is a set of practices for helping entrepreneurs increase their odds of building a successful startup. To set the record straight, it's important to define what a startup is:

> A startup is a human institution designed to create a new product or service under conditions of extreme uncertainty.

I've come to realize that the most important part of this definition is what it omits. It says nothing about size of the company, the industry, or the sector of the economy. Anyone who is creating a new product or business under conditions of extreme uncertainty is an entrepreneur whether he or she knows it or not and whether working in a government agency, a venture-backed company, a nonprofit, or a decidedly for-profit company with financial investors.

Let's take a look at each of the pieces. The word *institution* connotes bureaucracy, process, even lethargy. How can that be part of a startup? Yet successful startups are full of activities associated with building an institution: hiring creative employees, coordinating their activities, and creating a company culture that delivers results.

We often lose sight of the fact that a startup is not just about a product, a technological breakthrough, or even a brilliant idea. A startup is greater than the sum of its parts; it is an acutely human enterprise.

The fact that a startup's product or service is a new innovation is also an essential part of the definition and a tricky part too. I prefer to use the broadest definition of *product,* one that encompasses any source of value for the people who become customers. Anything those customers experience from their interaction with a company should be considered part of that company's product. This is true of a grocery store, an e-commerce website, a consulting service, and a nonprofit social service agency. In every case, the organization is dedicated to uncovering a new source of value for customers and cares about the impact of its product on those customers.

It's also important that the word *innovation* be understood broadly. Startups use many kinds of innovation: novel scientific discoveries, repurposing an existing technology for a new use, devising a new business model that unlocks value that was hidden, or simply bringing a product or service to a new location or a previously underserved set of customers. In all these cases, innovation is at the heart of the company's success.

There is one more important part of this definition: the context in which the innovation happens. Most businesses—large and small alike—are excluded from this context. Startups are designed to confront situations of extreme uncertainty. To open up a new business that is an exact clone of an existing business all the way down to the business model, pricing, target customer, and product may be an attractive economic investment, but it is not a startup because its success depends only on execution—so much so that this success can be modeled with high accuracy. (This is why so many small businesses can be financed with simple bank loans; the level of risk and uncertainty is understood well enough that a loan officer can assess its prospects.)

Most tools from general management are not designed to flourish in the harsh soil of extreme uncertainty in which startups thrive. The future is unpredictable, customers face a growing array of alternatives, and the pace of change is ever increasing. Yet most startups—in garages and enterprises alike—still are managed by using standard forecasts, product milestones, and detailed business plans.

THE SNAPTAX STORY

In 2009, a startup decided to try something really audacious. They wanted to liberate taxpayers from expensive tax stores by automating the process of collecting information typically found on W-2 forms (the end-of-year statement that most employees receive from their employer that summarizes their taxable wages for the year). The startup quickly ran into difficulties. Even though many consumers had access to a printer/scanner in their home or office, few knew how to use those devices. After numerous conversations with potential customers, the team lit upon the idea of having customers take photographs of the forms directly from their cell phone. In the process of testing this concept, customers asked something unexpected: would it be possible to finish *the whole tax return* right on the phone itself?

That was not an easy task. Traditional tax preparation requires consumers to wade through hundreds of questions, many forms, and a lot of paperwork. This startup tried something novel by deciding to ship an early version of its product that could do much less than a complete tax package. The initial version worked only for consumers with a very simple return to file, and it worked only in California.

Instead of having consumers fill out a complex form, they allowed the customers to use the phone's camera to take a picture of their W-2 forms. From that single picture, the company developed the technology to compile and file most of the 1040 EZ tax return. Compared with the drudgery of traditional tax filing, the new product—called SnapTax—provides a magical experience. From its modest beginning, SnapTax grew into a significant startup success story. Its nationwide launch in 2011 showed that customers loved it, to the tune of more than 350,000 downloads in the first three weeks.

This is the kind of amazing innovation you'd expect from a new startup.

However, the name of this company may surprise you. SnapTax was developed by Intuit, America's largest producer of finance, tax, and accounting tools for individuals and small businesses. With more than 7,700 employees and annual revenues in the billions, Intuit is not a typical startup.[2]

The team that built SnapTax doesn't look much like the archetypal image of entrepreneurs either. They don't work in a garage or eat ramen noodles. Their company doesn't lack for resources. They are paid a full salary and benefits. They come into a regular office every day. Yet they are entrepreneurs.

Stories like this one are not nearly as common inside large corporations as they should be. After all, SnapTax competes directly with one of Intuit's flagship products: the fully featured TurboTax desktop software. Usually, companies like Intuit fall into the trap described in Clayton Christensten's *The Innovator's Dilemma:* they are very good at creating incremental improvements to existing products and serving existing customers, which Christensen called *sustaining innovation*, but struggle to create breakthrough new products—*disruptive innovation*—that can create new sustainable sources of growth.

One remarkable part of the SnapTax story is what the team leaders said when I asked them to account for their unlikely success. Did they hire superstar entrepreneurs from outside the company? No, they assembled a team from within Intuit. Did they face constant meddling from senior management, which is the bane of innovation teams in many companies? No, their executive sponsors created an "island of freedom" where they could experiment as necessary. Did they have a huge team, a large budget, and lots of marketing dollars? Nope, they started with a team of five.

What allowed the SnapTax team to innovate was not their genes, destiny, or astrological signs but a process deliberately facilitated by Intuit's senior management. Innovation is a bottoms-up, decentralized, and unpredictable thing, but that doesn't mean it cannot be managed. It can, but to do so requires a new management discipline, one that needs to be mastered not just by practicing entrepreneurs seeking to build the next big thing but also by the people who support them, nurture them, and hold them accountable. In other words, cultivating entrepreneurship is the responsibility of senior management. Today, a cutting-edge company such as Intuit can point to success stories like SnapTax because it has recognized the need for a new management paradigm. This is a realization that was years in the making.[3]

A SEVEN-THOUSAND-PERSON LEAN STARTUP

In 1983, Intuit's founder, the legendary entrepreneur Scott Cook, had the radical notion (with cofounder Tom Proulx) that personal accounting should happen by computer. Their success was far from inevitable; they faced numerous competitors, an uncertain future, and an initially tiny market. A decade later, the company went public and subsequently fended off well-publicized attacks from larger incumbents, including the software behemoth Microsoft. Partly with the help of famed venture capitalist John Doerr, Intuit became a fully diversified enterprise, a member of the Fortune 1000 that now provides dozens of market-leading products across its major divisions.

This is the kind of entrepreneurial success we're used to hearing about: a ragtag team of underdogs who eventually achieve fame, acclaim, and significant riches.

Flash-forward to 2002. Cook was frustrated. He had just tabulated ten years of data on all of Intuit's new product introductions and had concluded that the company was getting a measly return on its massive investments. Simply put, too many of its new products were failing. By traditional standards, Intuit is an extremely well-managed company, but as Scott dug into the root causes of those failures, he came to a difficult conclusion: the prevailing management paradigm he and his company had been practicing was inadequate to the problem of continuous innovation in the modern economy.

By fall 2009, Cook had been working to change Intuit's management culture for several years. He came across my early work on the Lean Startup and asked me to give a talk at Intuit. In Silicon Valley this is not the kind of invitation you turn down. I admit I was curious. I was still at the beginning of my Lean Startup journey and didn't have much appreciation for the challenges faced by a Fortune 1000 company like his.

My conversations with Cook and Intuit chief executive officer (CEO) Brad Smith were my initiation into the thinking of modern general managers, who struggle with entrepreneurship every bit as much as do venture capitalists and founders in a garage. To combat these challenges, Scott and Brad are going back to Intuit's roots. They are working to build entrepreneurship and risk taking into all their divisions.

For example, consider one of Intuit's flagship products. Because TurboTax does most of its sales around tax season in the United States, it used to have an extremely conservative culture. Over the course of the year, the marketing and product teams would conceive one major initiative that would be rolled out just in time for tax season. Now they test over five hundred different changes in a two-and-a-half-month tax season. They're running up to seventy different tests per week. The team can make a change live on its website on Thursday, run it over the weekend, read the results on Monday, and come to conclusions starting Tuesday; then they rebuild new tests on Thursday and launch the next set on Thursday night.

As Scott put it, "Boy, the amount of learning they get is just immense now. And what it does is develop entrepreneurs, because when you have only one test, you don't have entrepreneurs, you have politicians, because you have to sell. Out of a hundred good ideas, you've got to sell your idea. So you build up a society of politicians and salespeople. When you have five hundred tests you're running, then everybody's ideas can run. And then you create entrepreneurs who run and learn and can retest and relearn as opposed to a society of politicians. So we're trying to drive that throughout our organization, using examples which have nothing to do with high tech, like the website example. Every business today has a website. You don't have to be high tech to use fast-cycle testing."

This kind of change is hard. After all, the company has a significant number of existing customers who continue to demand exceptional service and investors who expect steady, growing returns.

Scott says,

> It goes against the grain of what people have been taught in business and what leaders have been taught. The problem isn't with the teams or the entrepreneurs. They love the chance to quickly get their baby out into the market. They love the chance to have the customer vote instead of the suits voting. The real issue is with the leaders and the middle managers. There are many business leaders who have been successful because of analysis. They think they're analysts, and their job is to do great planning and analyzing and have a plan.

The amount of time a company can count on holding on to market leadership to exploit its earlier innovations is shrinking, and this creates an imperative for even the most entrenched companies to invest in innovation. In fact, I believe a company's only sustainable path to long-term economic growth is to build an "innovation factory" that uses Lean Startup techniques to create disruptive innovations on a continuous basis. In other words, established companies need to figure out how to accomplish what Scott Cook did in 1983, but on an industrial scale and with an established cohort of managers steeped in traditional management culture.

Ever the maverick, Cook asked me to put these ideas to the test, and so I gave a talk that was simulcast to all seven thousand–plus Intuit employees during which I explained the theory of the Lean Startup, repeating my definition: an organization designed to create new products and services under conditions of extreme uncertainty.

What happened next is etched in my memory. CEO Brad Smith had been sitting next to me as I spoke. When I was done, he got up and said before all of Intuit's employees, "Folks, listen up. You heard Eric's definition of a startup. It has three parts, and we here at Intuit match *all three parts* of that definition."

Scott and Brad are leaders who realize that something new is needed in management thinking. Intuit is proof that this kind of thinking can work in established companies. Brad explained to me how they hold themselves accountable for their new innovation efforts by measuring two things: the number of customers using products that didn't exist three years ago and the percentage of revenue coming from offerings that did not exist three years ago.

Under the old model, it took an average of 5.5 years for a successful new product to start generating $50 million in revenue. Brad explained to me, "We've generated $50 million in offerings that did not exist twelve months ago in the last year. Now it's not one particular offering. It's a combination of a whole bunch of innovation happening, but that's the kind of stuff that's creating some energy for us, that we think we can truly short-circuit the ramp by killing things that don't make sense fast and doubling down on the ones that do." For a company as large as Intuit, these are modest results and early days. They have decades of legacy systems and legacy thinking to overcome. However, their leadership in adopting entrepreneurial management is starting to pay off.

Leadership requires creating conditions that enable employees to do the kinds of experimentation that entrepreneurship requires. For example, changes in TurboTax enabled the Intuit team to develop five hundred experiments per tax season. Before that, marketers with great ideas couldn't have done those tests even if they'd wanted to, because they didn't have a system in place through which to change the website rapidly. Intuit invested in systems that increased the speed at which tests could be built, deployed, and analyzed.

As Cook says, "Developing these experimentation systems is

the responsibility of senior management; they have to be put in by the leadership. It's moving leaders from playing Caesar with their thumbs up and down on every idea to—instead—putting in the culture and the systems so that teams can move and innovate at the speed of the experimentation system."

3
LEARN

As an entrepreneur, nothing plagued me more than the question of whether my company was making progress toward creating a successful business. As an engineer and later as a manager, I was accustomed to measuring progress by making sure our work proceeded according to plan, was high quality, and cost about what we had projected.

After many years as an entrepreneur, I started to worry about measuring progress in this way. What if we found ourselves building something that nobody wanted? In that case what did it matter if we did it on time and on budget? When I went home at the end of a day's work, the only things I knew for sure were that I had kept people busy and spent money that day. I hoped that my team's efforts took us closer to our goal. If we wound up taking a wrong turn, I'd have to take comfort in the fact that at least we'd learned something important.

Unfortunately, "learning" is the oldest excuse in the book for a failure of execution. It's what managers fall back on when they fail to achieve the results we promised. Entrepreneurs, under pressure to succeed, are wildly creative when it comes to demonstrating what we have learned. We can all tell a good story when our job, career, or reputation depends on it.

However, learning is cold comfort to employees who are following an entrepreneur into the unknown. It is cold comfort to the investors who allocate precious money, time, and energy to entrepreneurial teams. It is cold comfort to the organizations—large and small—that depend on entrepreneurial innovation to survive. You can't take learning to the bank; you can't spend it or invest it. You cannot give it to customers and cannot return it to limited partners. Is it any wonder that learning has a bad name in entrepreneurial and managerial circles?

Yet if the fundamental goal of entrepreneurship is to engage in organization building under conditions of extreme uncertainty, its most vital function is learning. We must learn the truth about which elements of our strategy are working to realize our vision and which are just crazy. We must learn what customers really want, not what they say they want or what we think they should want. We must discover whether we are on a path that will lead to growing a sustainable business.

In the Lean Startup model, we are rehabilitating learning with a concept I call *validated learning*. Validated learning is not after-the-fact rationalization or a good story designed to hide failure. It is a rigorous method for demonstrating progress when one is embedded in the soil of extreme uncertainty in which startups grow. Validated learning is the process of demonstrating empirically that a team has discovered valuable truths about a startup's present and future business prospects. It is more concrete, more accurate, and faster than market forecasting or classical business planning. It is the principal antidote to the lethal problem of achieving failure: successfully executing a plan that leads nowhere.

VALIDATED LEARNING AT IMVU

Let me illustrate this with an example from my career. Many audiences have heard me recount the story of IMVU's founding and the many mistakes we made in developing our first product. I'll now elaborate on one of those mistakes to illustrate validated learning clearly.

Those of us involved in the founding of IMVU aspired to be serious strategic thinkers. Each of us had participated in previous ventures that had failed, and we were loath to repeat that experience. Our main concerns in the early days dealt with the following questions: What should we build and for whom? What market could we enter and dominate? How could we build durable value that would not be subject to erosion by competition?[1]

Brilliant Strategy

We decided to enter the instant messaging (IM) market. In 2004, that market had hundreds of millions of consumers actively participating worldwide. However, the majority of the customers who were using IM products were not paying for the privilege. Instead, large media and portal companies such as AOL, Microsoft, and Yahoo! operated their IM networks as a loss leader for other services while making modest amounts of money through advertising.

IM is an example of a market that involves strong *network effects*. Like most communication networks, IM is thought to follow Metcalfe's law: the value of a network as a whole is proportional to the square of the number of participants. In other words, the more people in the network, the more valuable the network. This makes intuitive sense: the value to each participant is driven primarily by how many other people he or she can communicate with. Imagine a world in which you own the only telephone; it would have no value. Only when other people also have a telephone does it become valuable.

In 2004, the IM market was locked up by a handful of

incumbents. The top three networks controlled more than 80 percent of the overall usage and were in the process of consolidating their gains in market share at the expense of a number of smaller players.[2] The common wisdom was that it was more or less impossible to bring a new IM network to market without spending an extraordinary amount of money on marketing.

The reason for that wisdom is simple. Because of the power of network effects, IM products have high switching costs. To switch from one network to another, customers would have to convince their friends and colleagues to switch with them. This extra work for customers creates a barrier to entry in the IM market: with all consumers locked in to an incumbent's product, there are no customers left with whom to establish a beachhead.

At IMVU we settled on a strategy of building a product that would combine the large mass appeal of traditional IM with the high revenue per customer of three-dimensional (3D) video games and virtual worlds. Because of the near impossibility of bringing a new IM network to market, we decided to build an IM add-on product that would interoperate with the existing networks. Thus, customers would be able to adopt the IMVU virtual goods and avatar communication technology without having to switch IM providers, learn a new user interface, and—most important—bring their friends with them.

In fact, we thought this last point was essential. For the add-on product to be useful, customers would *have* to use it with their existing friends. Every communication would come embedded with an invitation to join IMVU. Our product would be inherently viral, spreading throughout the existing IM networks like an epidemic. To achieve that viral growth, it was important that our add-on product support as many of the existing IM networks as possible and work on all kinds of computers.

Six Months to Launch

With this strategy in place, my cofounders and I began a period of intense work. As the chief technology officer, it was my responsibility, among other things, to write the software that would support IM interoperability across networks. My cofounders and I worked for months, putting in crazy hours struggling to get our first product released. We gave ourselves a hard deadline of six months—180 days—to launch the product and attract our first paying customers. It was a grueling schedule, but we were determined to launch on time.

The add-on product was so large and complex and had so many moving parts that we had to cut a lot of corners to get it done on time. I won't mince words: the first version was terrible. We spent endless hours arguing about which bugs to fix and which we could live with, which features to cut and which to try to cram in. It was a wonderful and terrifying time: we were full of hope about the possibilities for success and full of fear about the consequences of shipping a bad product.

Personally, I was worried that the low quality of the product would tarnish my reputation as an engineer. People would think I didn't know how to build a quality product. All of us feared tarnishing the IMVU brand; after all, we were charging people money for a product that didn't work very well. We all envisioned the damning newspaper headlines: "Inept Entrepreneurs Build Dreadful Product."

As launch day approached, our fears escalated. In our situation, many entrepreneurial teams give in to fear and postpone the launch date. Although I understand this impulse, I am glad we persevered, since delay prevents many startups from getting the feedback they need. Our previous failures made us more afraid of another, even worse, outcome than shipping a bad product: building something that nobody wants. And so, teeth clenched and apologies at the ready, we released our product to the public.

Launch

And then—nothing happened! It turned out that our fears were unfounded, because nobody even tried our product. At first I was relieved because at least nobody was finding out how bad the product was, but soon that gave way to serious frustration. After all the hours we had spent arguing about which features to include and which bugs to fix, our value proposition was so far off that customers weren't getting far enough into the experience to find out how bad our design choices were. Customers wouldn't even download our product.

Over the ensuing weeks and months, we labored to make the product better. We brought in a steady flow of customers through our online registration and download process. We treated each day's customers as a brand-new report card to let us know how we were doing. We eventually learned how to change the product's positioning so that customers at least would download it. We were making improvements to the underlying product continuously, shipping bug fixes and new changes daily. However, despite our best efforts, we were able to persuade only a pathetically small number of people to buy the product.

In retrospect, one good decision we made was to set clear revenue targets for those early days. In the first month we intended to make $300 in total revenue, and we did—barely. Many friends and family members were asked (okay, begged). Each month our small revenue targets increased, first to $350 and then to $400. As they rose, our struggles increased. We soon ran out of friends and family; our frustration escalated. We were making the product better every day, yet our customers' behavior remained unchanged: they still wouldn't use it.

Our failure to move the numbers prodded us to accelerate our efforts to bring customers into our office for in-person interviews and usability tests. The quantitative targets created the motivation to engage in qualitative inquiry and guided us in the questions we asked; this is a pattern we'll see throughout this book.

I wish I could say that I was the one to realize our mistake and suggest the solution, but in truth, I was the last to admit the problem. In short, our entire strategic analysis of the market was utterly wrong. We figured this out empirically, through experimentation, rather than through focus groups or market research. Customers could not tell us what they wanted; most, after all, had never heard of 3D avatars. Instead, they revealed the truth through their action or inaction as we struggled to make the product better.

Talking to Customers

Out of desperation, we decided to talk to some potential customers. We brought them into our office, and said, "Try this new product; it's IMVU." If the person was a teenager, a heavy user of IM, or a tech early adopter, he or she would engage with us. In constrast, if it was a mainstream person, the response was, "Right. So exactly what would you like me to do?" We'd get nowhere with the mainstream group; they thought IMVU was too weird.

Imagine a seventeen-year-old girl sitting down with us to look at this product. She chooses her avatar and says, "Oh, this is really fun." She's customizing the avatar, deciding how she's going to look. Then we say, "All right, it's time to download the instant messaging add-on," and she responds, "What's that?"

"Well, it's this thing that interoperates with the instant messaging client." She's looking at us and thinking, "I've never heard of that, my friends have never heard of that, why do you want me to do that?" It required a lot of explanation; an instant messaging add-on was not a product category that existed in her mind.

But since she was in the room with us, we were able to talk her into doing it. She downloads the product, and then we say, "Okay, invite one of your friends to chat." And she says, "No way!" We say, "Why not?" And she says, "Well, I don't know if this thing is cool yet. You want me to risk inviting one of my friends? What are they going to think of me? If it sucks, they're going to think I suck, right?" And we say, "No, no, it's going to be so much fun once you get the person in there; it's a *social* product." She looks at us, her face filled with doubt; you can see that this is a deal breaker. Of course, the first time I had that experience, I said, "It's all right, it's just this one person, send her away and get me a new one." Then the second customer comes in and says the same thing. Then the third customer comes in, and it's the same thing. You start to see patterns, and no matter how stubborn you are, there's obviously something wrong.

Customers kept saying, "I want to use it by myself. I want to try it out first to see if it's really cool before I invite a friend." Our team was from the video game industry, so we understood what that meant: single-player mode. So we built a single-player version. We'd bring new customers into our office. They'd customize the avatar and download the product like before. Then they would go into single-player mode, and we'd say, "Play with your avatar and dress it up; check out the cool moves it can make." Followed by, "Okay, you did that by yourself; now it's time to invite one of your friends." You can see what's coming. They'd say, "No way! This isn't cool." And we'd say, "Well, we *told* you it wasn't going to be cool! What is the point of a single-player experience for a social product?" See, we thought we should get a gold star just for listening to our customers. Except our customers still didn't like the product. They would look at us and say, "Listen, old man, you don't understand. What is the deal with this crazy business of inviting friends before I know if it's cool?" It was a total deal breaker.

Out of further desperation, we introduced a feature called ChatNow that allows you to push a button and be randomly matched with somebody else anywhere in the world. The only thing you have in common is that you both pushed the button at the same time. All of a sudden, in our customer service tests, people were saying, "Oh, this is fun!"

So we'd bring them in, they'd use ChatNow, and maybe they would meet somebody they thought was cool. They'd say, "Hey, that guy was neat; I want to add him to my buddy list. Where's my buddy list?" And we'd say, "Oh, no, you don't want a new buddy list; you want to use your regular AOL buddy list." Remember, this was how we planned to harness the interoperability that would lead to network effects and viral growth. Picture the customer looking at us, asking, "What do you want me to do exactly?" And we'd say, "Well, just give the stranger your AIM screen name so you can put him on your buddy list." You could see their eyes go wide, and they'd say, "Are you kidding me? A stranger on my AIM buddy list?" To which we'd respond, "Yes; otherwise you'd have to download a whole new IM client with a new buddy list." And they'd say, "Do you have any idea how many IM clients I already run?"

"No. One or two, maybe?" That's how many clients each of us in the office used. To which the teenager would say, "Duh! I run eight." We had no idea how many instant messaging clients there were in the world.

We had the incorrect preconception that it's a challenge to learn new software and it's tricky to move your friends over to a new buddy list. Our customers revealed that this was nonsense.

We wanted to draw diagrams on the whiteboard that showed why our strategy was brilliant, but our customers didn't understand concepts like network effects and switching costs. If we tried to explain why they should behave the way we predicted, they'd just shake their heads at us, bewildered.

We had a mental model for how people used software that was years out of date, and so eventually, painfully, after dozens of meetings like that, it started to dawn on us that the IM add-on concept was fundamentally flawed.[3]

Our customers did not want an IM add-on; they wanted a stand-alone IM network. They did not consider having to learn how to use a new IM program a barrier; on the contrary, our early adopters used many different IM programs simultaneously. Our customers were not intimidated by the idea of having to take their friends with them to a new IM network; it turned out that they enjoyed that challenge. Even more surprising, our assumption that customers would want to use avatar-based IM primarily with their existing friends was also wrong. They wanted to make new friends, an activity that 3D avatars are particularly well suited to facilitating. Bit by bit, customers tore apart our seemingly brilliant initial strategy.

Throwing My Work Away

Perhaps you can sympathize with our situation and forgive my obstinacy. After all, it was my work over the prior months that needed to be thrown away. I had slaved over the software that was required to make our IM program interoperate with other networks, which was at the heart of our original strategy. When it came time to pivot and abandon that original strategy, almost all of my work—thousands of lines of code—was thrown out. I felt betrayed. I was a devotee of the latest in software development methods (known collectively as agile development), which promised to help drive waste out of product development. However, despite that, I had committed the biggest waste of all: building a product that our customers refused to use. That was *really* depressing.

I wondered: in light of the fact that my work turned out to be a waste of time and energy, would the company have been just as well off if I had spent the last six months on a beach sipping umbrella drinks? Had I really been needed? Would it have been better if I had not done any work at all?

There is, as I mentioned at the beginning of this chapter, always one last refuge for people aching to justify their own failure. I consoled myself that if we hadn't built this first product—mistakes and all—we never would have learned these important insights about customers. We never would have learned that our strategy was flawed. There is truth in this excuse: what we learned during those critical early months set IMVU on a path that would lead to our eventual breakout success.

For a time, this "learning" consolation made me feel better, but my relief was short-lived. Here's the question that bothered me most of all: if the goal of those months was to learn these important insights about customers, why did it take so long? How much of our effort contributed to the essential lessons we needed to learn? Could we have learned those lessons earlier if I hadn't been so focused on making the product "better" by adding features and fixing bugs?

VALUE VS. WASTE

In other words, which of our efforts are value-creating and which are wasteful? This question is at the heart of the lean manufacturing revolution; it is the first question any lean manufacturing adherent is trained to ask. Learning to see waste and then systematically eliminate it has allowed lean companies such as Toyota to dominate entire industries. In the world of software, the agile development methodologies I had practiced until that time had their origins in lean thinking. They were designed to eliminate waste too.

Yet those methods had led me down a road in which the majority of my team's efforts were wasted. Why?

The answer came to me slowly over the subsequent years. Lean thinking defines value as providing benefit to the customer; anything else is waste. In a manufacturing business, customers don't care how the product is assembled, only that it works correctly. But in a startup, who the customer is and what the customer might find valuable are unknown, part of the very uncertainty that is an essential part of the definition of a startup. I realized that as a startup, we needed a new definition of value. The real progress we had made at IMVU was what we had learned over those first months about what creates value for customers.

Anything we had done during those months that did not contribute to our learning was a form of waste. Would it have been possible to learn the same things with less effort? Clearly, the answer is yes.

For one thing, think of all the debate and prioritization of effort that went into features that customers would never discover. If we had shipped sooner, we could have avoided that waste. Also consider all the waste caused by our incorrect strategic assumptions. I had built interoperability for more than a dozen different IM clients and networks. Was this really necessary to test our assumptions? Could we have gotten the same feedback from our customers with half as many networks? With only three? With only one? Since the customers of all IM networks found our product equally unattractive, the level of learning would have been the same, but our effort would have been dramatically less.

Here's the thought that kept me up nights: did we have to

support any networks at all? Is it possible that we could have discovered how flawed our assumptions were without building anything? For example, what if we simply had offered customers the opportunity to download the product from us solely on the basis of its proposed features before building anything? Remember, almost no customers were willing to use our original product, so we wouldn't have had to do much apologizing when we failed to deliver. (Note that this is different from asking customers what they want. Most of the time customers don't know what they want in advance.) We could have conducted an experiment, offering customers the chance to try something and then measuring their behavior.

Such thought experiments were extremely disturbing to me because they undermined my job description. As the head of product development, I thought my job was to ensure the timely delivery of high-quality products and features. But if many of those features were a waste of time, what should I be doing instead? How could we avoid this waste?

I've come to believe that learning is the essential unit of progress for startups. The effort that is not absolutely necessary for learning what customers want can be eliminated. I call this *validated learning* because it is always demonstrated by positive improvements in the startup's core metrics. As we've seen, it's easy to kid yourself about what you think customers want. It's also easy to learn things that are completely irrelevant. Thus, validated learning is backed up by empirical data collected from real customers.

WHERE DO YOU FIND VALIDATION?

As I can attest, anybody who fails in a startup can claim that he or she has learned a lot from the experience. They can tell a compelling story. In fact, in the story of IMVU so far, you might have noticed something missing. Despite my claims that we learned a lot in those early months, lessons that led to our eventual success, I haven't offered any evidence to back that up. In hindsight, it's easy to make such claims and sound credible (and you'll see some evidence later in the book), but imagine us in IMVU's early months trying to convince investors, employees, family members, and most of all ourselves that we had not squandered our time and resources. What evidence did we have?

Certainly our stories of failure were entertaining, and we had fascinating theories about what we had done wrong and what we needed to do to create a more successful product. However, the proof did not come until we put those theories into practice and built subsequent versions of the product that showed superior results with actual customers.

The next few months are where the true story of IMVU begins, not with our brilliant assumptions and strategies and whiteboard gamesmanship but with the hard work of discovering what customers really wanted and adjusting our product and strategy to meet those desires. We adopted the view that our job was to find a synthesis between our vision and what customers would accept; it wasn't to capitulate to what customers thought they wanted or to tell customers what they ought to want.

As we came to understand our customers better, we were able to improve our products. As we did that, the fundamental metrics of our business changed. In the early days, despite our efforts to improve the product, our metrics were stubbornly flat. We treated each day's customers as a new report card. We'd pay attention to the percentage of new customers who exhibited product behaviors such as downloading and buying our product. Each day, roughly the same number of customers would buy the product, and that number was pretty close to zero despite the many improvements.

However, once we pivoted away from the original strategy, things started to change. Aligned with a superior strategy, our product development efforts became magically more productive—not because we were working harder but because we were working smarter, aligned with our customers' real needs. Positive changes in metrics became the quantitative validation that our learning was real. This was critically important because we could show our stakeholders—employees, investors, and ourselves—that we were making genuine progress, not deluding ourselves. It is also the right way to think about productivity in a startup: not in terms of how much stuff we are building but in terms of how much validated learning we're getting for our efforts.[4]

For example, in one early experiment, we changed our entire website, home page, and product registration flow to replace "avatar chat" with "3D instant messaging." New customers were split automatically between these two versions of the site; half saw one, and half saw the other. We were able to measure the difference in behavior between the two groups. Not only were the people in the experimental group more likely to sign up for the product, they were more likely to become long-term paying customers.

We had plenty of failed experiments too. During one period in which we believed that customers weren't using the product because they didn't understand its many benefits, we went so far as to pay customer service agents to act as virtual tour guides for new customers. Unfortunately, customers who got that VIP treatment were no more likely to become active or paying customers.

Even after ditching the IM add-on strategy, it still took months to understand *why* it hadn't worked. After our pivot and many failed experiments, we finally figured out this insight: customers wanted to use IMVU to make *new* friends online. Our customers intuitively grasped something that we were slow to realize. All the existing social products online were centered on customers' real-life identity. IMVU's avatar technology, however, was uniquely well suited to help people get to know each other online without compromising safety or opening themselves up to identity theft. Once we formed this hypothesis, our experiments became much more likely to produce positive results. Whenever we would change the product to make it easier for people to find and keep new friends, we discovered that customers were more likely to engage. This is true startup productivity: systematically figuring out the right things to build.

These were just a few experiments among hundreds that we ran week in and week out as we started to learn which customers would use the product and why. Each bit of knowledge we gathered suggested new experiments to run, which moved our metrics closer and closer to our goal.

THE AUDACITY OF ZERO

Despite IMVU's early success, our gross numbers were still pretty small. Unfortunately, because of the traditional way businesses are evaluated, this is a dangerous situation. The irony is that it is often easier to raise money or acquire other resources when you have zero revenue, zero customers, and zero traction than when you have a small amount. Zero invites imagination, but small numbers invite questions about whether large numbers will ever materialize. Everyone knows (or thinks he or she knows) stories of products that achieved breakthrough success overnight. As long as nothing has been released and no data have been collected, it is still possible to imagine overnight success in the future. Small numbers pour cold water on that hope.

This phenomenon creates a brutal incentive: postpone getting any data until you are certain of success. Of course, as we'll see, such delays have the unfortunate effect of increasing the amount of wasted work, decreasing essential feedback, and dramatically increasing the risk that a startup will build something nobody wants.

However, releasing a product and hoping for the best is not a good plan either, because this incentive is real. When we launched IMVU, we were ignorant of this problem. Our earliest investors and advisers thought it was quaint that we had a $300-per-month revenue plan at first. But after several months with our revenue hovering around $500 per month, some began to lose faith, as did some of our advisers, employees, and even spouses. In fact, at one point, some investors were seriously recommending that we pull the product out of the market and return to stealth mode. Fortunately, as we pivoted and experimented, incorporating what we learned into our product development and marketing efforts, our numbers started to improve.

But not by much! On the one hand, we were lucky to see a growth pattern that started to look like the famous hockey stick graph. On the other hand, the graph went up only to a few thousand dollars per month. These early graphs, although promising, were not by themselves sufficient to combat the loss of faith caused by our early failure, and we lacked the language of validated learning to provide an alternative concept to rally around. We were quite fortunate that some of our early investors understood its importance and were willing to look beyond our small gross numbers to see the real progress we were making. (You'll see the exact same graphs they did in Chapter 7.)

Thus, we can mitigate the waste that happens because of the audacity of zero with validated learning. What we needed to demonstrate was that our product development efforts were leading us toward massive success without giving in to the temptation to fall back on vanity metrics and "success theater"—the work we do to make ourselves look successful. We could have tried marketing gimmicks, bought a Super Bowl ad, or tried flamboyant public relations (PR) as a way of juicing our gross numbers. That would have given investors the illusion of traction, but only for a short time. Eventually, the fundamentals of the business would win out and the PR bump would pass. Because we would have squandered precious resources on theatrics instead of progress, we would have been in real trouble.

Sixty million avatars later, IMVU is still going strong. Its legacy is not just a great product, an amazing team, and promising financial results but a whole new way of measuring the progress of startups.

LESSONS BEYOND IMVU

I have had many opportunities to teach the IMVU story as a business case ever since Stanford's Graduate School of Business wrote an official study about IMVU's early years.[5] The case is now part of the entrepreneurship curriculum at several business schools, including Harvard Business School, where I serve as an entrepreneur in residence. I've also told these stories at countless workshops, lectures, and conferences.

Every time I teach the IMVU story, students have an overwhelming temptation to focus on the tactics it illustrates: launching a low-quality early prototype, charging customers from day one, and using low-volume revenue targets as a way to drive accountability. These are useful techniques, but they are not the moral of the story. There are too many exceptions. Not every kind of customer will accept a low-quality prototype, for example. If the students are more skeptical, they may argue that the techniques do not apply to their industry or situation, but work only because IMVU is a software company, a consumer Internet business, or a non-mission-critical application.

None of these takeaways is especially useful. The Lean Startup is not a collection of individual tactics. It is a principled approach to new product development. The only way to make sense of its recommendations is to understand the underlying principles that make them work. As we'll see in later chapters, the Lean Startup model has been applied to a wide variety of businesses and industries: manufacturing, clean tech, restaurants, and even laundry. The tactics from the IMVU story may or may not make sense in your particular business.

Instead, the way forward is to learn to see every startup in any industry as a grand experiment. The question is not "Can this product be built?" In the modern economy, almost any product that can be imagined can be built. The more pertinent questions are "Should this product be built?" and "Can we build a sustainable business around this set of products and services?" To answer those questions, we need a method for systematically breaking down a business plan into its component parts and testing each part empirically.

In other words, we need the scientific method. In the Lean Startup model, every product, every feature, every marketing campaign—everything a startup does—is understood to be an experiment designed to achieve validated learning. This experimental approach works across industries and sectors, as we'll see in Chapter 4.

4
EXPERIMENT

I come across many startups that are struggling to answer the following questions: Which customer opinions should we listen to, if any? How should we prioritize across the many features we could build? Which features are essential to the product's success and which are ancillary? What can be changed safely, and what might anger customers? What might please today's customers at the expense of tomorrow's? What should we work on next?

These are some of the questions teams struggle to answer if they have followed the "let's just ship a product and see what happens" plan. I call this the "just do it" school of entrepreneurship after Nike's famous slogan.[1] Unfortunately, if the plan is to see what happens, a team is guaranteed to succeed—at seeing what happens—but won't necessarily gain validated learning. This is one of the most important lessons of the scientific method: if you cannot fail, you cannot learn.

FROM ALCHEMY TO SCIENCE

The Lean Startup methodology reconceives a startup's efforts as experiments that test its strategy to see which parts are brilliant and which are crazy. A true experiment follows the scientific method. It begins with a clear hypothesis that makes predictions about what is supposed to happen. It then tests those predictions empirically. Just as scientific experimentation is informed by theory, startup experimentation is guided by the startup's vision. The goal of every startup experiment is to discover how to build a sustainable business around that vision.

Think Big, Start Small

Zappos is the world's largest online shoe store, with annual gross sales in excess of $1 billion. It is known as one of the most successful, customer-friendly e-commerce businesses in the world, but it did not start that way.

Founder Nick Swinmurn was frustrated because there was no central online site with a great selection of shoes. He envisioned a new and superior retail experience. Swinmurn could have waited a long time, insisting on testing his complete vision complete with warehouses, distribution partners, and the promise of significant sales. Many early e-commerce pioneers did just that, including infamous dot-com failures such as Webvan and Pets.com.

Instead, he started by running an experiment. His hypothesis was that customers were ready and willing to buy shoes online. To test it, he began by asking local shoe stores if he could take pictures of their inventory. In exchange for permission to take the pictures, he would post the pictures online and come back to buy the shoes at full price if a customer bought them online.

Zappos began with a tiny, simple product. It was designed to answer one question above all: is there already sufficient demand for a superior online shopping experience for shoes? However, a well-designed startup experiment like the one Zappos began with does more than test a single aspect of a business plan. In the course of testing this first assumption, many other assumptions were tested as well. To sell the shoes, Zappos had to interact with customers: taking payment, handling returns, and dealing with customer support. This is decidedly different from market research. If Zappos had relied on existing market research or conducted a survey, it could have asked what customers thought they wanted. By building a product instead, albeit a simple one, the company learned much more:

1. It had more accurate data about customer demand because it was observing real customer behavior, not asking hypothetical questions.
2. It put itself in a position to interact with real customers and learn about their needs. For example, the business plan might call for discounted pricing, but how are customer perceptions of the product affected by the discounting strategy?
3. It allowed itself to be surprised when customers behaved in unexpected ways, revealing information Zappos might not have known to ask about. For example, what if customers returned the shoes?

Zappos' initial experiment provided a clear, quantifiable outcome: either a sufficient number of customers would buy the shoes or they would not. It also put the company in a position to observe, interact with, and learn from real customers and partners. This qualitative learning is a necessary companion to quantitative testing. Although the early efforts were decidedly small-scale, that did not prevent the huge Zappos vision from being realized. In fact, in 2009 Zappos was acquired by the e-commerce giant Amazon.com for a reported $1.2 billion.[2]

For Long-Term Change, Experiment Immediately

Caroline Barlerin is a director in the global social innovation division at Hewlett-Packard (HP), a multinational company with more than three hundred thousand employees and more than $100 billion in annual sales. Caroline, who leads global community involvement, is a social entrepreneur working to get more of HP's employees to take advantage of the company's policy on volunteering.

Corporate guidelines encourage every employee to spend up to four hours a month of company time volunteering in his or her community; that volunteer work could take the form of any philanthropic effort: painting fences, building houses, or even using pro bono or work-based skills outside the company. Encouraging the latter type of volunteering was Caroline's priority. Because of its talent and values, HP's combined workforce has the potential to have a monumental positive impact. A designer could help a nonprofit with a new website design. A team of engineers could wire a school for Internet access.

Caroline's project is just beginning, and most employees do not know that this volunteering policy exists, and only a tiny fraction take advantage of it. Most of the volunteering has been of the low-impact variety, involving manual labor, even when the volunteers were highly trained experts. Barlerin's vision is to take the hundreds of thousands of employees in the company and transform them into a force for social good.

This is the kind of corporate initiative undertaken every day at companies around the world. It doesn't look like a startup by the conventional definition or what we see in the movies. On the surface it seems to be suited to traditional management and planning. However, I hope the discussion in Chapter 2 has prompted you to be a little suspicious. Here's how we might analyze this project using the Lean Startup framework.

Caroline's project faces extreme uncertainty: there had never been a volunteer campaign of this magnitude at HP before. How confident should she be that she knows the real reasons people aren't volunteering? Most important, how much does she really know about how to change the behavior of hundreds of thousand people in more than 170 countries? Barlerin's goal is to inspire her colleagues to make the world a better place. Looked at that way, her plan seems full of untested assumptions—and a lot of vision.

In accordance with traditional management practices, Barlerin is spending time planning, getting buy-in from various departments and other managers, and preparing a road map of initiatives for the first eighteen months of her project. She also has a strong accountability framework with metrics for the impact her project should have on the company over the next four years. Like many entrepreneurs, she has a business plan that lays out her intentions nicely. Yet despite all that work, she is—so far—creating one-off wins and no closer to knowing if her vision will be able to scale.

One assumption, for example, might be that the company's long-standing values included a commitment to improving the community but that recent economic trouble had resulted in an increased companywide strategic focus on short-term profitability. Perhaps longtime employees would feel a desire to reaffirm their values of giving back to the community by volunteering. A second assumption could be that they would find it more satisfying and therefore more sustainable to use their actual workplace skills in a volunteer capacity, which would have a greater impact on behalf of the organizations to which they donated their time. Also lurking within Caroline's plans are many practical assumptions about employees' willingness to take the time to volunteer, their level of commitment and desire, and the way to best reach them with her message.

The Lean Startup model offers a way to test these hypotheses rigorously, immediately, and thoroughly. Strategic planning takes months to complete; these experiments could begin immediately. By starting small, Caroline could prevent a tremendous amount of waste down the road without compromising her overall vision. Here's what it might look like if Caroline were to treat her project as an experiment.

Break It Down

The first step would be to break down the grand vision into its component parts. The two most important assumptions entrepreneurs make are what I call the value hypothesis and the growth hypothesis.

The *value hypothesis* tests whether a product or service really delivers value to customers once they are using it. What's a good indicator that employees find donating their time valuable? We could survey them to get their opinion, but that would not be very accurate because most people have a hard time assessing their feelings objectively.

Experiments provide a more accurate gauge. What could we see in real time that would serve as a proxy for the value participants were gaining from volunteering? We could find opportunities for a small number of employees to volunteer and then look at the retention rate of those employees. How many of them sign up to volunteer again? When an employee voluntarily invests their time and attention in this program, that is a strong indicator that they find it valuable.

For the *growth hypothesis,* which tests how new customers will discover a product or service, we can do a similar analysis. Once the program is up and running, how will it spread among the employees, from initial early adopters to mass adoption throughout the company? A likely way this program could expand is through viral growth. If that is true, the most important thing to measure is behavior: would the early participants actively spread the word to other employees?

In this case, a simple experiment would involve taking a very small number—a dozen, perhaps—of existing long-term employees and providing an exceptional volunteer opportunity for them. Because Caroline's hypothesis was that employees would be motivated by their desire to live up to HP's historical commitment to community service, the experiment would target employees who felt the greatest sense of disconnect between their daily routine and the company's expressed values. The point is not to find the average customer but to find *early adopters:* the customers who feel the need for the product most acutely. Those customers tend to be more forgiving of mistakes and are especially eager to give feedback.

Next, using a technique I call the *concierge minimum viable product* (described in detail in Chapter 6), Caroline could make sure the first few participants had an experience that was as good as she could make it, completely aligned with her vision. Unlike in a focus group, her goal would be to measure what the customers actually did. For example, how many of the first volunteers actually complete their volunteer assignments? How many volunteer a second time? How many are willing to recruit a colleague to participate in a subsequent volunteer activity?

Additional experiments can expand on this early feedback and learning. For example, if the growth model requires that a certain percentage of participants share their experiences with colleagues and encourage their participation, the degree to which that takes place can be tested even with a very small sample of people. If ten people complete the first experiment, how many do we expect to volunteer again? If they are asked to recruit a colleague, how many do we expect will do so? Remember that these are supposed to be the kinds of early adopters with the most to gain from the program.

Put another way, what if all ten early adopters decline to volunteer again? That would be a highly significant—and very negative—result. If the numbers from such early experiments don't look promising, there is clearly a problem with the strategy. That doesn't mean it's time to give up; on the contrary, it means it's time to get some immediate qualitative feedback about how to improve the program. Here's where this kind of experimentation has an advantage over traditional market research. We don't have to commission a survey or find new people to interview. We already have a cohort of people to talk to as well as knowledge about their actual behavior: the participants in the initial experiment.

This entire experiment could be conducted in a matter of weeks, less than one-tenth the time of the traditional strategic planning process. Also, it can happen in parallel with strategic planning while the plan is still being formulated. Even when experiments produce a negative result, those failures prove instructive and can influence the strategy. For example, what if no volunteers can be found who are experiencing the conflict of values within the organization that was such an important assumption in the business plan? If so, congratulations: it's time to pivot (a concept that is explored in more detail in Chapter 8).[3]

AN EXPERIMENT IS A PRODUCT

In the Lean Startup model, an experiment is more than just a theoretical inquiry; it is also a first product. If this or any other experiment is successful, it allows the manager to get started with his or her campaign: enlisting early adopters, adding employees to each further experiment or iteration, and eventually starting to build a product. By the time that product is ready to be distributed widely, it will already have established customers. It will have solved real problems and offer detailed specifications for what needs to be built. Unlike a traditional strategic planning or market research process, this specification will be rooted in feedback on what is working today rather than in anticipation of what might work tomorrow.

To see this in action, consider an example from Kodak. Kodak's history is bound up with cameras and film, but today it also operates a substantial online business called Kodak Gallery. Mark Cook is Kodak Gallery's vice president of products, and he is working to change Kodak Gallery's culture of development to embrace experimentation.

Mark explained, "Traditionally, the product manager says, 'I just want this.' In response, the engineer says, 'I'm going to build it.' Instead, I try to push my team to first answer four questions:

1. Do consumers recognize that they have the problem you are trying to solve?
2. If there was a solution, would they buy it?
3. Would they buy it from us?
4. Can we build a solution for that problem?"

The common tendency of product development is to skip straight to the fourth question and build a solution before confirming that customers have the problem. For example, Kodak Gallery offered wedding cards with gilded text and graphics on its site. Those designs were popular with customers who were getting married, and so the team redesigned the cards to be used at other special occasions, such as for holidays. The market research and design process indicated that customers would like the new cards, and that finding justified the significant effort that went into creating them.

Days before the launch, the team realized the cards were too difficult to understand from their depiction on the website; people couldn't see how beautiful they were. They were also hard to produce. Cook realized that they had done the work backward. He explained, "Until we could figure out how to sell and make the product, it wasn't worth spending any engineering time on."

Learning from that experience, Cook took a different approach when he led his team through the development of a new set of features for a product that makes it easier to share photos taken at an event. They believed that an online "event album" would provide a way for people who attended a wedding, a conference, or another gathering to share photos with other attendees. Unlike other online photo sharing services, Kodak Gallery's event album would have strong privacy controls, assuring that the photos would be shared only with people who attended the same event.

In a break with the past, Cook led the group through a process of identifying risks and assumptions before building anything and then testing those assumptions experimentally.

There were two main hypotheses underlying the proposed event album:

1. The team assumed that customers would want to create the albums in the first place.
2. It assumed that event participants would upload photos to event albums created by friends or colleagues.

The Kodak Gallery team built a simple prototype of the event album. It lacked many features—so many, in fact, that the team was reluctant to show it to customers. However, even at that early stage, allowing customers to use the prototype helped the team refute their hypotheses. First, creating an album was not as easy as the team had predicted; *none* of the early customers were able to create one. Further, customers complained that the early product version lacked essential features.

Those negative results demoralized the team. The usability problems frustrated them, as did customer complains about missing features, many of which matched the original road map. Cook explained that even though the product was missing features, the project was not a failure. The initial product—flaws and all—confirmed that users did have the desire to create event albums, which was extremely valuable information. Where customers complained about missing features, this suggested that the team was on the right track. The team now had early evidence that those features were in fact important. What about features that were on the road map but that customers didn't complain about? Maybe those features weren't as important as they initially seemed.

Through a beta launch the team continued to learn and iterate. While the early users were enthusiastic and the numbers were promising, the team made a major discovery. Through the use of online surveying tool KISSinsights, the team learned that many customers wanted to be able to arrange the order of pictures before they would invite others to contribute. Knowing they weren't ready to launch, Cook held off his division's general manager by explaining how iterating and experimenting before beginning the marketing campaign would yield far better results. In a world where marketing launch dates were often set months in advance, waiting until the team had really solved the problem was a break from the past.

This process represented a dramatic change for Kodak Gallery; employees were used to being measured on their progress at completing tasks. As Cook says, "Success is not delivering a feature; success is learning how to solve the customer's problem."[4]

THE VILLAGE LAUNDRY SERVICE

In India, due to the cost of a washing machine, less than seven percent of the population have one in their homes. Most people either hand wash their clothing at home or pay a Dhobi to do it for them. Dhobis take the clothes to the nearest river, wash them in the river water, bang them against rocks to get them clean, and hang them to dry, which takes two to seven days. The result? Clothes are returned in about ten days and are probably not that clean.

Akshay Mehra had been working at Procter & Gamble Singapore for eight years when he sensed an opportunity. As the brand manager of the Tide and Pantene brands for India and ASEAN countries, he thought he could make laundry services available to people who previously could not afford them. Returning to India, Akshay joined the Village Laundry Services (VLS), created by Innosight Ventures. VLS began a series of experiments to test its business assumptions.

For their first experiment, VLS mounted a consumer-grade laundry machine on the back of a pickup truck parked on a street corner in Bangalore. The experiment cost less than $8,000 and had the simple goal of proving that people would hand over their laundry and pay to have it cleaned. The entrepreneurs did not clean the laundry on the truck, which was more for marketing and show, but took it off-site to be cleaned and brought it back to their customers by the end of the day.

The VLS team continued the experiment for a week, parking the truck on different street corners, digging deeper to discover all they could about their potential customers. They wanted to know how they could encourage people to come to the truck. Did cleaning speed matter? Was cleanliness a concern? What were people asking for when they left their laundry with them?

They discovered that customers were happy to give them their laundry to clean. However, those customers were suspicious of the washing machine mounted on the back of the truck, concerned that VLS would take their laundry and run. To address that concern, VLS created a slightly more substantial mobile cart that looked more like a kiosk.

VLS also experimented with parking the carts in front of a local minimarket chain. Further iterations helped VLS figure out which services people were most interested in and what price they were willing to pay. They discovered that customers often wanted their clothes ironed and were willing to pay double the price to get their laundry back in four hours rather than twenty-four hours.

As a result of those early experiments, VLS created an end product that was a three-foot by four-foot mobile kiosk that included an energy-efficient, consumer-grade washing machine, a dryer, and an extra-long extension cord. The kiosk used Western detergents and was supplied daily with fresh clean water delivered by VLS.

Since then, the Village Laundry Service has grown substantially, with fourteen locations operational in Bangalore, Mysore, and Mumbai. As CEO Akshay Mehra shared with me, "We have serviced 116,000 kgs. in 2010 (vs. 30,600 kg. in 2009). And almost 60 percent of the business is coming from repeat customers. We have serviced more than 10,000 customers in the past year alone across all the outlets."[5]

A LEAN STARTUP IN GOVERNMENT?

On July 21, 2010, President Obama signed the Dodd–Frank Wall Street Reform and Consumer Protection Act into law. One of its landmark provisions created a new federal agency, the

Consumer Federal Protection Bureau (CFPB). This agency is tasked with protecting American citizens from predatory lending by financial services companies such as credit card companies, student lenders, and payday loan offices. The plan calls for it to accomplish this by setting up a call center where trained case workers will field calls directly from the public.

Left to its own devices, a new government agency would probably hire a large staff with a large budget to develop a plan that is expensive and time-consuming. However, the CFPB is considering doing things differently. Despite its $500 million budget and high-profile origins, the CPFB is really a startup.

President Obama tasked his chief technology officer, Aneesh Chopra, with collecting ideas for how to set up the new startup agency, and that is how I came to be involved. On one of Chopra's visits to Silicon Valley, he invited a number of entrepreneurs to make suggestions for ways to cultivate a startup mentality in the new agency. In particular, his focus was on leveraging technology and innovation to make the agency more efficient, cost-effective, and thorough.

My suggestion was drawn straight from the principles of this chapter: treat the CFPB as an experiment, identify the elements of the plan that are assumptions rather than facts, and figure out ways to test them. Using these insights, we could build a minimum viable product and have the agency up and running—on a micro scale—long before the official plan was set in motion.

The number one assumption underlying the current plan is that once Americans know they can call the CFPB for help with financial fraud and abuse, there will be a significant volume of citizens who do that. This sounds reasonable, as it is based on market research about the amount of fraud that affects Americans each year. However, despite all that research, it is still an assumption. If the actual call volume differs markedly from that in the plan, it will require significant revision. What if Americans who are subjected to financial abuse don't view themselves as victims and therefore don't seek help? What if they have very different notions of what problems are important? What if they call the agency seeking help for problems that are outside its purview?

Once the agency is up and running with a $500 million budget and a correspondingly large staff, altering the plan will be expensive and time-consuming, but why wait to get feedback? To start experimenting immediately, the agency could start with the creation of a simple hotline number, using one of the new breed of low-cost and fast setup platforms such as Twilio. With a few hours' work, they could add simple voice prompts, offering callers a menu of financial problems to choose from. In the first version, the prompts could be drawn straight from the existing research. Instead of a caseworker on the line, each prompt could offer the caller useful information about how to solve her or his problem.

Instead of marketing this hotline to the whole country, the agency could run the experiment in a much more limited way: start with a small geographic area, perhaps as small as a few city blocks, and instead of paying for expensive television or radio advertising to let people know about the service, use highly targeted advertising. Flyers on billboards, newspaper advertisements to those blocks, or specially targeted online ads would be a good start. Since the target area is so small, they could afford to pay a premium to create a high level of awareness in the target zone. The total cost would remain quite small.

As a comprehensive solution to the problem of financial abuse, this minimum viable product is not very good compared with what a $500 million agency could accomplish. But it is also not very expensive. This product could be built in a matter of days or weeks, and the whole experiment probably would cost only a few thousand dollars.

What we would learn from this experiment would be invaluable. On the basis of the selections of those first callers, the agency could immediately start to get a sense of what kinds of problems Americans believe they have, not just what they "should" have. The agency could begin to test marketing messages: What motivates people to call? It could start to extrapolate real-world trends: What percentage of people in the target area actually call? The extrapolation would not be perfect, but it would establish a baseline behavior that would be far more accurate than market research.

Most important, this product would serve as a seed that could germinate into a much more elaborate service. With this beginning, the agency could engage in a continuous process of improvement, slowly but surely adding more and better solutions. Eventually, it would staff the hotline with caseworkers, perhaps at first addressing only one category of problems, to give the caseworkers the best chance of success. By the time the official plan was ready for implementation, this early service could serve as a real-world template.

The CFPB is just getting started, but already they are showing signs of following an experimental approach. For example, instead of doing a geographically limited rollout, they are segmenting their first products by use case. They have established a preliminary order of financial products to provide consumer services for, with credit cards coming first. As their first experiment unfolds, they will have the opportunity to closely monitor all of the other complaints and consumer feedback they receive. This data will influence the depth, breadth, and sequence of future offerings.

As David Forrest, the CFPB's chief technology officer, told me, "Our goal is to give American citizens an easy way to tell us about the problems they see out there in the consumer financial marketplace. We have an opportunity to closely monitor what the public is telling us and react to new information. Markets change all the time and our job is to change with them."[6]

○ ○ ○

The entrepreneurs and managers profiled in this book are smart, capable, and extremely results-oriented. In many cases, they are in the midst of building an organization in a way consistent with the best practices of current management thinking. They face the same challenges in both the public and private sectors, regardless of industry. As we've seen, even the seasoned managers and executives at the world's best-run companies struggle to consistently develop and launch innovative new products.

Their challenge is to overcome the prevailing management thinking that puts its faith in well-researched plans. Remember, planning is a tool that only works in the presence of a long and stable operating history. And yet, do any of us feel that the world around us is getting more and more stable every day? Changing such a mind-set is hard but critical to startup success. My hope is that this book will help managers and entrepreneurs make this change.

Part Two
STEER

How Vision Leads to Steering

At its heart, a startup is a catalyst that transforms ideas into products. As customers interact with those products, they generate feedback and data. The feedback is both qualitative (such as what they like and don't like) and quantitative (such as how many people use it and find it valuable). As we saw in Part One, the products a startup builds are really experiments; the learning about how to build a sustainable business is the outcome of those experiments. For startups, that information is much more important than dollars, awards, or mentions in the press, because it can influence and reshape the next set of ideas.

We can visualize this three-step process with this simple diagram:

BUILD-MEASURE-LEARN FEEDBACK LOOP

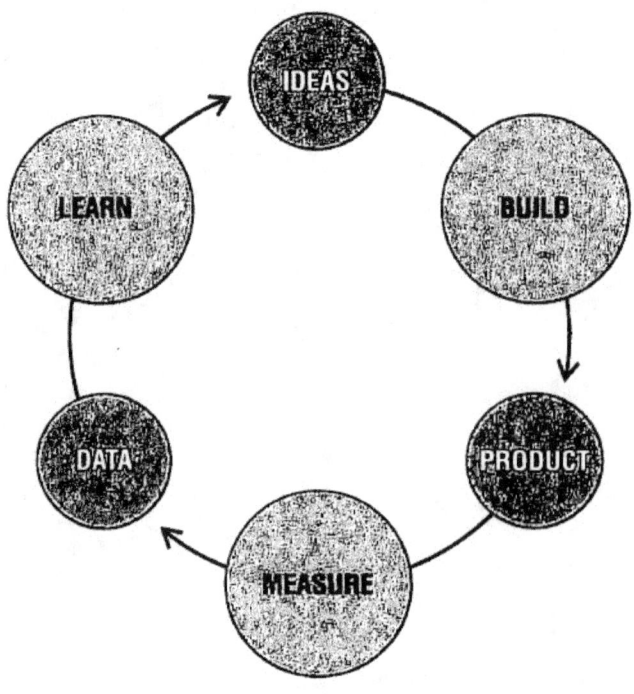

Minimize *TOTAL* time through the loop

This Build-Measure-Learn feedback loop is at the core of the Lean Startup model. In Part Two, we will examine it in great detail.

Many people have professional training that emphasizes one element of this feedback loop. For engineers, it's learning to build things as efficiently as possible. Some managers are experts at strategizing and learning at the whiteboard. Plenty of entrepreneurs focus their energies on the individual nouns: having the best product idea or the best-designed initial product or obsessing over data and metrics. The truth is that none of these activities by itself is of paramount importance. Instead, we need to focus our energies on minimizing the *total* time through this feedback loop. This is the essence of steering a startup and is the subject of Part Two. We will walk through a complete turn of the Build-Measure-Learn feedback loop, discussing each of the components in detail.

The purpose of Part One was to explore the importance of learning as the measure of progress for a startup. As I hope is evident by now, by focusing our energies on validated learning, we can avoid much of the waste that plagues startups today. As in lean manufacturing, learning where and when to invest energy results in saving time and money.

To apply the scientific method to a startup, we need to identify which hypotheses to test. I call the riskiest elements of a startup's plan, the parts on which everything depends, *leap-of-faith* assumptions. The two most important assumptions are the value hypothesis and the growth hypothesis. These give rise to tuning variables that control a startup's engine of growth. Each iteration of a startup is an attempt to rev this engine to see if it will turn. Once it is running, the process repeats, shifting into higher and higher gears.

Once clear on these leap-of-faith assumptions, the first step is to enter the Build phase as quickly as possible with a minimum viable product (MVP). The MVP is that version of the product that enables a full turn of the Build-Measure-Learn loop with a minimum amount of effort and the least amount of development time. The minimum viable product lacks many features that may prove essential later on. However, in some ways, creating a MVP requires extra work: we must be able to measure its impact. For example, it is inadequate to build a prototype that is evaluated solely for internal quality by engineers and designers. We also need to get it in front of potential customers to gauge their reactions. We may even need to try selling them the prototype, as we'll soon see.

When we enter the Measure phase, the biggest challenge will be determining whether the product development efforts are leading to real progress. Remember, if we're building something that nobody wants, it doesn't much matter if we're doing it on time and on budget. The method I recommend is called *innovation accounting*, a quantitative approach that allows us to see whether our engine-tuning efforts are bearing fruit. It also allows us to create *learning milestones*, which are an alternative to traditional business and product milestones. Learning milestones are useful for entrepreneurs as a way of assessing their progress accurately and objectively; they are also invaluable to managers and investors who must hold entrepreneurs accountable. However, not all metrics are created equal, and in Chapter 7 I'll clarify the danger of *vanity metrics* in contrast to the nuts-and-bolts usefulness of *actionable metrics*, which help to analyze customer behavior in ways that support innovation accounting.

Finally, and most important, there's the *pivot*. Upon completing the Build-Measure-Learn loop, we confront the most difficult question any entrepreneur faces: whether to pivot the original strategy or persevere. If we've discovered that one of our hypotheses is false, it is time to make a major change to a new strategic hypothesis.

The Lean Startup method builds capital-efficient companies because it allows startups to recognize that it's time to pivot sooner, creating less waste of time and money. Although we write the feedback loop as Build-Measure-Learn because the activities happen in that order, our planning really works in the reverse order: we figure out what we need to learn, use innovation accounting to figure out what we need to measure to know if we are gaining validated learning, and then figure out what product we need to build to run that experiment and get that measurement. All of the techniques in Part Two are designed to minimize the total time through the Build-Measure-Learn feedback loop.

5
LEAP

In 2004, three college sophomores arrived in Silicon Valley with their fledgling college social network. It was live on a handful of college campuses. It was not the market-leading social network or even the first college social network; other companies had launched sooner and with more features. With 150,000 registered users, it made very little revenue, yet that summer they raised their first $500,000 in venture capital. Less than a year later, they raised an additional $12.7 million.

Of course, by now you've guessed that these three college sophomores were Mark Zuckerberg, Dustin Moskovitz, and Chris Hughes of Facebook. Their story is now world famous. Many things about it are remarkable, but I'd like to focus on only one: how Facebook was able to raise so much money when its actual usage was so small.[1]

By all accounts, what impressed investors the most were two facts about Facebook's early growth. The first fact was the raw amount of time Facebook's active users spent on the site. More than half of the users came back to the site every single day.[2] This is an example of how a company can validate its value hypothesis—that customers find the product valuable. The second impressive thing about Facebook's early traction was the rate at which it had taken over its first few college campuses. The rate of growth was staggering: Facebook launched on February 4, 2004, and by the end of that month almost three-quarters of Harvard's undergraduates were using it, without a dollar of marketing or advertising having been spent. In other words, Facebook also had validated its growth hypothesis. These two hypotheses represent two of the most important *leap-of-faith* questions any new startup faces.[3]

At the time, I heard many people criticize Facebook's early investors, claiming that Facebook had "no business model" and only modest revenues relative to the valuation offered by its investors. They saw in Facebook a return to the excesses of the dot-com era, when companies with little revenue raised massive amounts of cash to pursue a strategy of "attracting eyeballs" and "getting big fast." Many dot-com-era startups planned to make money later by selling the eyeballs they had bought to other advertisers. In truth, those dot-com failures were little more than middlemen, effectively paying money to acquire customers' attention and then planning to resell it to others. Facebook was different, because it employed a different engine of growth. It paid nothing for customer acquisition, and its high engagement meant that it was accumulating massive amounts of customer attention every day. There was never any question that attention would be valuable to advertisers; the only question was how much they would pay.

Many entrepreneurs are attempting to build the next Facebook, yet when they try to apply the lessons of Facebook and other famous startup success stories, they quickly get confused. Is the lesson of Facebook that startups should not charge customers money in the early days? Or is it that startups should never spend money on marketing? These questions cannot be answered in the abstract; there are an almost infinite number of counterexamples for any technique. Instead, as we saw in Part One, startups need to conduct experiments that help determine what techniques will work in their unique circumstances. For startups, the role of strategy is to help figure out the right questions to ask.

STRATEGY IS BASED ON ASSUMPTIONS

Every business plan begins with a set of assumptions. It lays out a strategy that takes those assumptions as a given and proceeds to show how to achieve the company's vision. Because the assumptions haven't been proved to be true (they are assumptions, after all) and in fact are often erroneous, the goal of a startup's early efforts should be to test them as quickly as possible.

What traditional business strategy excels at is helping managers identify clearly what assumptions are being made in a particular business. The first challenge for an entrepreneur is to build an organization that can test these assumptions systematically. The second challenge, as in all entrepreneurial situations, is to perform that rigorous testing without losing sight of the company's overall vision.

Many assumptions in a typical business plan are unexceptional. These are well-established facts drawn from past industry experience or straightforward deductions. In Facebook's case, it was clear that advertisers would pay for customers' attention. Hidden among these mundane details are a handful of assumptions that require more courage to state—in the present tense—with a straight face: we assume that customers have a significant desire to use a product like ours, or we assume that supermarkets will carry our product. Acting as if these assumptions are true is a classic entrepreneur superpower. They are called *leaps of faith* precisely because the success of the entire venture rests on them. If they are true, tremendous opportunity awaits. If they are false, the startup risks total failure.

Most leaps of faith take the form of an argument by analogy. For example, one business plan I remember argued as follows: "Just as the development of progressive image loading allowed the widespread use of the World Wide Web over dial-up, so too our progressive rendering technology will allow our product to run on low-end personal computers." You probably have no idea what progressive image loading or rendering is, and it doesn't much matter. But you know the argument (perhaps you've even used it):

Previous technology X was used to win market Y because of attribute Z. We have a new technology X2 that will enable us to win market Y2 because we too have attribute Z.

The problem with analogies like this is that they obscure the true leap of faith. That is their goal: to make the business seem less risky. They are used to persuade investors, employees, or partners to sign on. Most entrepreneurs would cringe to see their leap of faith written this way:

Large numbers of people already wanted access to the World Wide Web. They knew what it was, they could afford it, but they could not get access to it because the time it took to load images was too long. When progressive image loading was introduced, it allowed people to get onto the World Wide Web and tell their friends about it. Thus, company X won market Y.
Similarly, there is already a large number of potential customers who want access to our product right now. They know they want it, they can afford it, but they cannot access it because the rendering is too slow. When we debut our product with progressive rendering technology,

they will flock to our software and tell their friends, and we will win market Y2.

There are several things to notice in this revised statement. First, it's important to identify the facts clearly. Is it really true that progressive image loading caused the adoption of the World Wide Web, or was this just one factor among many? More important, is it really true that there are large numbers of potential customers out there who want our solution right now? The earlier analogy was designed to convince stakeholders that a reasonable first step is to build the new startup's technology and see if customers will use it. The restated approach should make clear that what is needed is to do some empirical testing first: let's make sure that there really are hungry customers out there eager to embrace our new technology.

Analogs and Antilogs

There is nothing intrinsically wrong with basing strategy on comparisons to other companies and industries. In fact, that approach can help you discover assumptions that are not really leaps of faith. For example, the venture capitalist Randy Komisar, whose book *Getting to Plan B* discussed the concept of leaps of faith in great detail, uses a framework of "analogs" and "antilogs" to plot strategy.

He explains the analog-antilog concept by using the iPod as an example. "If you were looking for analogs, you would have to look at the Walkman," he says. "It solved a critical question that Steve Jobs never had to ask himself: Will people listen to music in a public place using earphones? We think of that as a nonsense question today, but it is fundamental. When Sony asked the question, they did not have the answer. Steve Jobs had [the answer] in the analog [version]" Sony's Walkman was the analog. Jobs then had to face the fact that although people were willing to download music, they were not willing to pay for it. "Napster was an antilog. That antilog had to lead him to address his business in a particular way," Komisar says. "Out of these analogs and antilogs come a series of unique, unanswered questions. Those are leaps of faith that I, as an entrepreneur, am taking if I go through with this business venture. They are going to make or break my business. In the iPod business, one of those leaps of faith was that people would pay for music." Of course that leap of faith turned out to be correct.[4]

Beyond "The Right Place at the Right Time"

There are any number of famous entrepreneurs who made millions because they seemed to be in the right place at the right time. However, for every successful entrepreneur who was in the right place in the right time, there are many more who were there, too, in that right place at the right time but still managed to fail. Henry Ford was joined by nearly five hundred other entrepreneurs in the early twentieth century. Imagine being an automobile entrepreneur, trained in state-of-the-art engineering, on the ground floor of one of the biggest market opportunities in history. Yet the vast majority managed to make no money at all.[5] We saw the same phenomenon with Facebook, which faced early competition from other college-based social networks whose head start proved irrelevant.

What differentiates the success stories from the failures is that the successful entrepreneurs had the foresight, the ability, and the tools to discover which parts of their plans were working brilliantly and which were misguided, and adapt their strategies accordingly.

Value and Growth

As we saw in the Facebook story, two leaps of faith stand above all others: the value creation hypothesis and the growth hypothesis. The first step in understanding a new product or service is to figure out if it is fundamentally value-creating or value-destroying. I use the language of economics in referring to value rather than profit, because entrepreneurs include people who start not-for-profit social ventures, those in public sector startups, and internal change agents who do not judge their success by profit alone. Even more confusing, there are many organizations that are wildly profitable in the short term but ultimately value-destroying, such as the organizers of Ponzi schemes, and fraudulent or misguided companies (e.g., Enron and Lehman Brothers).

A similar thing is true for growth. As with value, it's essential that entrepreneurs understand the reasons behind a startup's growth. There are many value-destroying kinds of growth that should be avoided. An example would be a business that grows through continuous fund-raising from investors and lots of paid advertising but does not develop a value-creating product.

Such businesses are engaged in what I call success theater, using the appearance of growth to make it seem that they are successful. One of the goals of innovation accounting, which is discussed in depth in Chapter 7, is to help differentiate these false startups from true innovators. Traditional accounting judges new ventures by the same standards it uses for established companies, but these indications are not reliable predictors of a startup's future prospects. Consider companies such as Amazon.com that racked up huge losses on their way to breakthrough success.

Like its traditional counterpart, innovation accounting requires that a startup have and maintain a quantitative financial model that can be used to evaluate progress rigorously. However, in a startup's earliest days, there is not enough data to make an informed guess about what this model might look like. A startup's earliest strategic plans are likely to be hunch- or intuition-guided, and that is a good thing. To translate those instincts into data, entrepreneurs must, in Steve Blank's famous phrase, "get out of the building" and start learning.

GENCHI GEMBUTSU

The importance of basing strategic decisions on firsthand understanding of customers is one of the core principles that underlies the Toyota Production System. At Toyota, this goes by the Japanese term *genchi gembutsu*, which is one of the most important phrases in the lean manufacturing vocabulary. In English, it is usually translated as a directive to "go and see for yourself" so that business decisions can be based on deep firsthand knowledge. Jeffrey Liker, who has extensively documented the "Toyota Way," explains it this way:

> In my Toyota interviews, when I asked what distinguishes the Toyota Way from other management approaches, the most common first response was *genchi gembutsu*—whether I was in manufacturing, product development, sales, distribution, or public affairs. You cannot be sure you really understand any part of any business problem unless you go and see for yourself firsthand. It is unacceptable to take anything for granted or to rely on the reports of others.[6]

To demonstrate, take a look at the development of Toyota's Sienna minivan for the 2004 model year. At Toyota, the manager responsible for the design and development of a new model is called the chief engineer, a cross-functional leader who oversees the entire process from concept to production. The 2004 Sienna was assigned to Yuji Yokoya, who had very little experience in North America, which was the Sienna's primary market. To figure out how to improve the minivan, he proposed an audacious entrepreneurial undertaking: a road trip spanning all fifty U.S. states, all thirteen provinces and territories of Canada, and all parts of Mexico. In all, he logged more than 53,000 miles of driving. In small towns and large cities, Yokoya would rent a current-model Sienna, driving it in addition to talking to and observing real customers. From those firsthand observations, Yokoya was able to start testing his critical assumptions about what North American consumers wanted in a minivan.

It is common to think of selling to consumers as easier than selling to enterprises, because customers lack the complexity of multiple departments and different people playing different roles in the purchasing process. Yokoya discovered this was untrue for his customers: "The parents and grandparents may own the minivan. But it's the kids who rule it. It's the kids who occupy the rear two-thirds of the vehicle. And it's the kids who are the most critical—and the most appreciative of their environment. If I learned anything in my travels, it was the new Sienna would need kid appeal."[7] Identifying these assumptions helped guide the car's development. For example, Yokoya spent an unusual amount of the Sienna's development budget on internal comfort features, which are critical to a long-distance family road trip (such trips are much more common in America than in Japan).

The results were impressive, boosting the Sienna's market share dramatically. The 2004 model's sales were 60 percent higher than those in 2003. Of course, a product like the Sienna is a classic *sustaining innovation*, the kind that the world's best-managed established companies, such as Toyota, excel at. Entrepreneurs face a different set of challenges because they operate with much higher uncertainty. While a company working on a sustaining innovation knows enough about who and where their customers are to use *genchi gembutsu* to discover what customers want, startups' early contact with potential customers merely reveals what assumptions require the most urgent testing.

GET OUT OF THE BUILDING

Numbers tell a compelling story, but I always remind entrepreneurs that metrics are people, too. No matter how many intermediaries lie between a company and its customers, at the end of the day, customers are breathing, thinking, buying individuals. Their behavior is measurable and changeable. Even when one is selling to large institutions, as in a business-to-business model, it helps to remember that those businesses are made up of individuals. All successful sales models depend on breaking down the monolithic view of organizations into the disparate people that make them up.

As Steve Blank has been teaching entrepreneurs for years, the facts that we need to gather about customers, markets, suppliers, and channels exist only "outside the building." Startups need extensive contact with potential customers to understand them, so get out of your chair and get to know them.

The first step in this process is to confirm that your leap-of-faith questions are based in reality, that the customer has a significant problem worth solving.[8] When Scott Cook conceived Intuit in 1982, he had a vision—at that time quite radical—that someday consumers would use personal computers to pay bills and keep track of expenses. When Cook left his consulting job to take the entrepreneurial plunge, he didn't start with stacks of market research or in-depth analysis at the whiteboard. Instead, he picked up two phone books: one for Palo Alto, California, where he was living at the time, and the other for Winnetka, Illinois.

Calling people at random, he inquired if he could ask them a few questions about the way they managed their finances. Those early conversations were designed to answer this leap-of-faith question: do people find it frustrating to pay bills by hand? It turned out that they did, and this early validation gave Cook the confirmation he needed to get started on a solution.[9]

Those early conversations did not delve into the product features of a proposed solution; that attempt would have been foolish. The average consumers at that time were not conversant enough with personal computers to have an opinion about whether they'd want to use them in a new way. Those early conversations were with mainstream customers, not early adopters. Still, the conversations yielded a fundamental insight: if Intuit could find a way to solve this problem, there could be a large mainstream audience on which it could build a significant business.

Design and the Customer Archetype

The goal of such early contact with customers is not to gain definitive answers. Instead, it is to clarify at a basic, coarse level that we understand our potential customer and what problems they have. With that understanding, we can craft a *customer archetype*, a brief document that seeks to humanize the proposed target customer. This archetype is an essential guide for product development and ensures that the daily prioritization decisions that every product team must make are aligned with the customer to whom the company aims to appeal.

There are many techniques for building an accurate customer archetype that have been developed over long years of practice in the design community. Traditional approaches such as interaction design or design thinking are enormously helpful. To me, it has always seemed ironic that many of these approaches are highly experimental and iterative, using techniques such as rapid prototyping and in-person customer observations to guide designers' work. Yet because of the way design agencies traditionally have been compensated, all this work culminates in a monolithic deliverable to the client. All of a sudden, the rapid learning and experimentation stops; the assumption is that the designers have learned all there is to know. For startups, this is an unworkable model. No amount of design can anticipate the many complexities of bringing a product to life in the real world.

In fact, a new breed of designers is developing brand-new techniques under the banner of Lean User Experience (Lean UX). They recognize that the customer archetype is a hypothesis, not a fact. The customer profile should be considered provisional until the strategy has shown via validated learning that we can serve this type of customer in a sustainable way.[10]

ANALYSIS PARALYSIS

There are two ever-present dangers when entrepreneurs conduct market research and talk to customers. Followers of the just-do-it school of entrepreneurship are impatient to get started and don't want to spend time analyzing their strategy. They'd rather start building immediately, often after just a few cursory customer conversations. Unfortunately, because customers don't really know what they want, it's easy for these entrepreneurs to delude themselves that they are on the right path.

Other entrepreneurs can fall victim to analysis paralysis,

endlessly refining their plans. In this case, talking to customers, reading research reports, and whiteboard strategizing are all equally unhelpful. The problem with most entrepreneurs' plans is generally not that they don't follow sound strategic principles but that the facts upon which they are based are wrong. Unfortunately, most of these errors cannot be detected at the whiteboard because they depend on the subtle interactions between products and customers.

If too much analysis is dangerous but none can lead to failure, how do entrepreneurs know when to stop analyzing and start building? The answer is a concept called the minimum viable product, the subject of Chapter 6.

6
TEST

Groupon is one of the fastest-growing companies of all time. Its name comes from "group coupons," an ingenious idea that has spawned an entire industry of social commerce imitators. However, it didn't start out successful. When customers took Groupon up on its first deal, a whopping twenty people bought two-for-one pizza in a restaurant on the first floor of the company's Chicago offices—hardly a world-changing event.

In fact, Groupon wasn't originally meant to be about commerce at all. The founder, Andrew Mason, intended his company to become a "collective activism platform" called The Point. Its goal was to bring people together to solve problems they couldn't solve on their own, such as fund-raising for a cause or boycotting a certain retailer. The Point's early results were disappointing, however, and at the end of 2008 the founders decided to try something new. Although they still had grand ambitions, they were determined to keep the new product simple. They built a minimum viable product. Does this sound like a billion-dollar company to you? Mason tells the story:

> We took a WordPress Blog and we skinned it to say Groupon and then every day we would do a new post. It was totally ghetto. We would sell T-shirts on the first

version of Groupon. We'd say in the write-up, "This T-shirt will come in the color red, size large. If you want a different color or size, e-mail that to us." We didn't have a form to add that stuff. It was just so cobbled together.

It was enough to prove the concept and show that it was something that people really liked. The actual coupon generation that we were doing was all FileMaker. We would run a script that would e-mail the coupon PDF to people. It got to the point where we'd sell 500 sushi coupons in a day, and we'd send 500 PDFs to people with Apple Mail at the same time. Really until July of the first year it was just a scrambling to grab the tiger by the tail. It was trying to catch up and reasonably piece together a product.[1]

Handmade PDFs, a pizza coupon, and a simple blog were enough to launch Groupon into record-breaking success; it is on pace to become the fastest company in history to achieve $1 billion in sales. It is revolutionizing the way local businesses find new customers, offering special deals to consumers in more than 375 cities worldwide.[2]

○ ○ ○

A minimum viable product (MVP) helps entrepreneurs start the process of learning as quickly as possible.[3] It is not necessarily the smallest product imaginable, though; it is simply the fastest way to get through the Build-Measure-Learn feedback loop with the minimum amount of effort.

Contrary to traditional product development, which usually involves a long, thoughtful incubation period and strives for product perfection, the goal of the MVP is to begin the process of learning, not end it. Unlike a prototype or concept test, an

MVP is designed not just to answer product design or technical questions. Its goal is to test fundamental business hypotheses.

WHY FIRST PRODUCTS AREN'T MEANT TO BE PERFECT

At IMVU, when we were raising money from venture investors, we were embarrassed. First of all, our product was still buggy and low-quality. Second, although we were proud of our business results, they weren't exactly earth-shattering. The good news was that we were on a hockey-stick-shaped growth curve. The bad news was that the hockey stick went up to only about $8,000 per month of revenue. These numbers were so low that we'd often have investors ask us, "What are the units on these charts? Are those numbers in thousands?" We'd have to reply, "No, sir, those are in ones."

However, those early results were extremely significant in predicting IMVU's future path. As you'll see in Chapter 7, we were able to validate two of our leap-of-faith assumptions: IMVU was providing value for customers, and we had a working engine of growth. The gross numbers were small because we were selling the product to visionary early customers called *early adopters*. Before new products can be sold successfully to the mass market, they have to be sold to early adopters. These people are a special breed of customer. They accept—in fact prefer—an 80 percent solution; you don't need a perfect solution to capture their interest.[4]

Early technology adopters lined up around the block for Apple's original iPhone even though it lacked basic features such as copy and paste, 3G Internet speed, and support for corporate e-mail. Google's original search engine could answer queries about specialized topics such as Stanford University and the Linux operating system, but it would be years before it could "organize the world's information." However, this did not stop early adopters from singing its praises.

Early adopters use their imagination to fill in what a product is missing. They prefer that state of affairs, because what they care about above all is being the first to use or adopt a new product or technology. In consumer products, it's often the thrill of being the first one on the block to show off a new basketball shoe, music player, or cool phone. In enterprise products, it's often about gaining a competitive advantage by taking a risk with something new that competitors don't have yet. Early adopters are suspicious of something that is too polished: if it's ready for everyone to adopt, how much advantage can one get by being early? As a result, additional features or polish beyond what early adopters demand is a form of wasted resources and time.

This is a hard truth for many entrepreneurs to accept. After all, the vision entrepreneurs keep in their heads is of a high-quality mainstream product that will change the world, not one used by a small niche of people who are willing to give it a shot before it's ready. That world-changing product is polished, slick, and ready for prime time. It wins awards at trade shows and, most of all, is something you can proudly show Mom and Dad. An early, buggy, incomplete product feels like an unacceptable compromise. How many of us were raised with the expectation that we would put our best work forward? As one manager put it to me recently, "I know for me, the MVP feels a little dangerous—in a good way—since I have always been such a perfectionist."

Minimum viable products range in complexity from extremely simple smoke tests (little more than an advertisement) to actual early prototypes complete with problems and missing features. Deciding exactly how complex an MVP needs to be cannot be done formulaically. It requires judgment. Luckily, this judgment is not difficult to develop: most entrepreneurs and product development people dramatically overestimate how many features are needed in an MVP. When in doubt, simplify.

For example, consider a service sold with a one-month free trial. Before a customer can use the service, he or she has to sign up for the trial. One obvious assumption, then, of the business model is that customers will sign up for a free trial once they have a certain amount of information about the service. A critical question to consider is whether customers will in fact sign up for the free trial given a certain number of promised features (the value hypothesis).

Somewhere in the business model, probably buried in a single cell in a spreadsheet, it specifies the "percentage of customers who see the free trial offer who then sign up." Maybe in our projections we say that this number should be 10 percent. If you think about it, this is a leap-of-faith question. It really should be represented in giant letters in a bold red font: WE ASSUME 10 PERCENT OF CUSTOMERS WILL SIGN UP.

Most entrepreneurs approach a question like this by building the product and then checking to see how customers react to it. I consider this to be exactly backward because it can lead to a lot of waste. First, if it turns out that we're building something nobody wants, the whole exercise will be an avoidable expense of time and money. If customers won't sign up for the free trial, they'll never get to experience the amazing features that await them. Even if they do sign up, there are many other opportunities for waste. For example, how many features do we really need to include to appeal to early adopters? Every extra feature is a form of waste, and if we delay the test for these extra features, it comes with a tremendous potential cost in terms of learning and cycle time.

The lesson of the MVP is that any additional work beyond

what was required to start learning is waste, no matter how important it might have seemed at the time.

To demonstrate, I'll share several MVP techniques from actual Lean Startups. In each case, you'll witness entrepreneurs avoiding the temptation to overbuild and overpromise.

THE VIDEO MINIMUM VIABLE PRODUCT

Drew Houston is the CEO of Dropbox, a Silicon Valley company that makes an extremely easy-to-use file-sharing tool. Install its application, and a Dropbox folder appears on your computer desktop. Anything you drag into that folder is uploaded automatically to the Dropbox service and then instantly replicated across all your computers and devices.

The founding team was made up of engineers, as the product demanded significant technical expertise to build. It required, for example, integration with a variety of computer platforms and operating systems: Windows, Macintosh, iPhone, Android, and so on. Each of these implementations happens at a deep level of the system and requires specialized know-how to make the user experience exceptional. In fact, one of Dropbox's biggest competitive advantages is that the product works in such a seamless way that the competition struggles to emulate it.

These are not the kind of people one would think of as marketing geniuses. In fact, none of them had ever worked in a marketing job. They had prominent venture capital backers and could have been expected to apply the standard engineering thinking to building the business: build it and they will come. But Dropbox did something different.

In parallel with their product development efforts, the founders wanted feedback from customers about what really mattered to them. In particular, Dropbox needed to test its leap-of-faith question: if we can provide a superior customer experience, will people give our product a try? They believed—rightly, as it turned out—that file synchronization was a problem that most people didn't know they had. Once you experience the solution, you can't imagine how you ever lived without it.

This is not the kind of entrepreneurial question you can ask or expect an answer to in a focus group. Customers often don't know what they want, and they often had a hard time understanding Dropbox when the concept was explained. Houston learned this the hard way when he tried to raise venture capital. In meeting after meeting, investors would explain that this "market space" was crowded with existing products, none of them had made very much money, and the problem wasn't a very important one. Drew would ask: "Have you personally tried those other products?" When they would say yes, he'd ask: "Did they work seamlessly for you?" The answer was almost always no. Yet in meeting after meeting, the venture capitalists could not imagine a world in line with Drew's vision. Drew, in contrast, believed that if the software "just worked like magic," customers would flock to it.

The challenge was that it was impossible to demonstrate the working software in a prototype form. The product required that they overcome significant technical hurdles; it also had an online service component that required high reliability and availability. To avoid the risk of waking up after years of development with a product nobody wanted, Drew did something unexpectedly easy: he made a video.

The video is banal, a simple three-minute demonstration of the technology as it is meant to work, but it was targeted at a community of technology early adopters. Drew narrates the video personally, and as he's narrating, the viewer is watching his screen. As he describes the kinds of files he'd like to synchronize, the viewer can watch his mouse manipulate his computer. Of course, if you're paying attention, you start to notice that the files he's moving around are full of in-jokes and humorous references that were appreciated by this community of early adopters. Drew recounted, "It drove hundreds of thousands of people to the website. Our beta waiting list went from 5,000 people to 75,000 people literally overnight. It totally blew us away." Today, Dropbox is one of Silicon Valley's hottest companies, rumored to be worth more than $1 billion.[5]

In this case, the video was the minimum viable product. The MVP validated Drew's leap-of-faith assumption that customers wanted the product he was developing not because they said so in a focus group or because of a hopeful analogy to another business, but because they actually signed up.

THE CONCIERGE MINIMUM VIABLE PRODUCT

Consider another kind of MVP technique: the *concierge MVP*. To understand how this technique works, meet Manuel Rosso, the CEO of an Austin, Texas–based startup called Food on the Table. Food on the Table creates weekly meal plans and grocery lists that are based on food you and your family enjoy, then hooks into your local grocery stores to find the best deals on the ingredients.

After you sign up for the site, you walk through a little setup in which you identify your main grocery store and check off the foods your family likes. Later, you can pick another nearby store if you want to compare prices. Next, you're presented with a list of items that are based on your preferences and asked: "What are you in the mood for this week?" Make your choices, select the number of meals you're ready to plan, and choose what you care about most in terms of time, money, health, or variety. At this point, the site searches through recipes that match your needs, prices out the cost of the meal for you, and lets you print out your shopping list.[6]

Clearly, this is an elaborate service. Behind the scenes, a team of professional chefs devise recipes that take advantage of items that are on sale at local grocery stores around the country. Those recipes are matched via computer algorithm to each family's unique needs and preferences. Try to visualize the work involved: databases of almost every grocery store in the country must be maintained, including what's on sale at each one this week. Those groceries have to be matched to appropriate recipes and then appropriately customized, tagged, and sorted. If a recipe calls for broccoli rabe, is that the same ingredient as the broccoli on sale at the local market?

After reading that description, you might be surprised to learn that Food on the Table (FotT) began life with a single customer. Instead of supporting thousands of grocery stores around the country as it does today, FotT supported just one. How did the company choose which store to support? The founders didn't—until they had their first customer. Similarly, they began life with no recipes whatsoever—until their first customer was ready to begin her meal planning. In fact, the company served its first customer without building any software, without signing any business development partnerships, and without hiring any chefs.

Manuel, along with VP of product Steve Sanderson, went to local supermarkets and moms' groups in his hometown of Austin. Part of their mission was the typical observation of customers that is a part of design thinking and other ideation techniques. However, Manuel and his team were also on the hunt for something else: their first customer.

As they met potential customers in those settings, they would interview them the way any good market researcher would, but at the end of each interview they would attempt to make a sale. They'd describe the benefits of FotT, name a weekly subscription fee, and invite the customer to sign up. Most times they were rejected. After all, most people are not early adopters and will not sign up for a new service sight unseen. But eventually someone did.

That one early adopter got the concierge treatment. Instead of interacting with the FotT product via impersonal software, she got a personal visit each week from the CEO of the company. He and the VP of product would review what was on sale at her preferred grocery store and carefully select recipes on the basis of her preferences, going so far as to learn her favorite recipes for items she regularly cooked for her family. Each week they would hand her—in person—a prepared packet containing a shopping list and relevant recipes, solicit her feedback, and make changes as necessary. Most important, each week they would collect a check for $9.95.

Talk about inefficient! Measured according to traditional criteria, this is a terrible system, entirely nonscalable and a complete waste of time. The CEO and VP of product, instead of building their business, are engaged in the drudgery of solving just one customer's problem. Instead of marketing themselves to millions, they sold themselves to one. Worst of all, their efforts didn't appear to be leading to anything tangible. They had no product, no meaningful revenue, no databases of recipes, not even a lasting organization.

However, viewed through the lens of the Lean Startup, they were making monumental progress. Each week they were learning more and more about what was required to make their product a success. After a few weeks they were ready for another customer. Each customer they brought on made it easier to get the next one, because FotT could focus on the same grocery store, getting to know its products and the kinds of people who shopped there well. Each new customer got the concierge treatment: personal in-home visits, the works. But after a few more customers, the overhead of serving them one-on-one started to increase.

Only at the point where the founders were too busy to bring on additional customers did Manuel and his team start to invest in automation in the form of product development. Each iteration of their minimum viable product allowed them to save a little more time and serve a few more customers: delivering the recipes and shopping list via e-mail instead of via an in-home visit, starting to parse lists of what was on sale automatically via software instead of by hand, even eventually taking credit card payments online instead of a handwritten check.

Before long, they had built a substantial service offering, first in the Austin area and eventually nationwide. But along the way, their product development team was always focused on scaling something that was working rather than trying to invent something that might work in the future. As a result, their development efforts involved far less waste than is typical for a venture of this kind.

It is important to contrast this with the case of a small business, in which it is routine to see the CEO, founder, president, and owner serving customers directly, one at a time. In a concierge MVP, this personalized service is not the product but a learning activity designed to test the leap-of-faith assumptions in the company's growth model. In fact, a common outcome of a concierge MVP is to invalidate the company's proposed growth model, making it clear that a different approach is needed. This can happen even if the initial MVP is profitable for the company. Without a formal growth model, many companies get caught in the trap of being satisfied with a small profitable business when a pivot (change in course or strategy) might lead to more significant growth. The only way to know is to have tested the growth model systematically with real customers.

PAY NO ATTENTION TO THE EIGHT PEOPLE BEHIND THE CURTAIN

Meet Max Ventilla and Damon Horowitz, technologists with a vision to build a new type of search software designed to answer the kinds of questions that befuddle state-of-the-art companies such as Google. Google befuddled? Think about it. Google and its peers excel at answering factual questions: What is the tallest mountain in the world? Who was the twenty-third president of the United States? But for more subjective questions, Google struggles. Ask, "What's a good place to go out for a drink after the ball game in my city?" and the technology flails. What's interesting about this class of queries is that they are relatively easy for a *person* to answer. Imagine being at a cocktail party surrounded by friends. How likely would you be to get a high-quality answer to your subjective question? You almost certainly would get one. Unlike factual queries, because these subjective questions have no single right answer, today's technology struggles to answer them. Such questions depend on the person answering them, his or her personal experience, taste, and assessment of what you're looking for.

To solve this problem, Max and Damon created a product called Aardvark. With their deep technical knowledge and industry experience, it would have been reasonable to expect them to dive in and start programming. Instead, they took six months to figure out what they should be building. But they didn't spend that year at the whiteboard strategizing or engage in a lengthy market research project.

Instead, they built a series of functioning products, each designed to test a way of solving this problem for their customers. Each product was then offered to beta testers, whose behavior was used to validate or refute each specific hypothesis (see examples in sidebar).

The following list of projects are examples from Aardvark's ideation period.[7]

Rekkit. A service to collect your ratings from across the web and give better recommendations to you.

Ninjapa. A way that you could open accounts in various applications through a single website and manage your data across multiple sites.

The Webb. A central number that you could call and talk to a person who could do anything for you that you could do online.

Web Macros. A way to record sequences of steps on websites so that you could repeat common actions, even across sites, and share "recipes" for how you accomplished online tasks.

Internet Button Company. A way to package steps taken on a website and smart form-fill functionality. People could encode buttons and share buttons à la social bookmarking.

Max and Damon had a vision that computers could be used to create a virtual personal assistant to which their customers could ask questions. Because the assistant was designed for subjective questions, the answers required human judgment. Thus, the early Aardvark experiments tried many variations on this theme, building a series of prototypes for ways customers could interact with the virtual assistant and get their questions answered. All the early prototypes failed to engage the customers.

As Max describes it, "We self-funded the company and released very cheap prototypes to test. What became Aardvark was the sixth prototype. Each prototype was a two- to four-week effort. We used humans to replicate the back end as much as possible. We invited one hundred to two hundred friends to try the prototypes and measured how many of them came back. The results were unambiguously negative until Aardvark."

Because of the short time line, none of the prototypes involved advanced technology. Instead, they were MVPs designed to test a more important question: what would be required to get customers to engage with the product and tell their friends about it?

"Once we chose Aardvark," Ventilla says, "we continued to run with humans replicating pieces of the backend for nine months. We hired eight people to manage queries, classify conversations, etc. We actually raised our seed and series A rounds before the system was automated—the assumption was that the lines between humans and artificial intelligence would cross, and we at least proved that we were building stuff people would respond to.

"As we refined the product, we would bring in six to twelve people weekly to react to mockups, prototypes, or simulations that we were working on. It was a mix of existing users and people who never saw the product before. We had our engineers join for many of these sessions, both so that they could make modifications in real time, but also so we could all experience the pain of a user not knowing what to do."[8]

The Aardvark product they settled on worked via instant messaging (IM). Customers could send Aardvark a question via IM, and Aardvark would get them an answer that was drawn from the customer's social network: the system would seek out the customer's friends and friends of friends and pose the question to them. Once it got a suitable answer, it would report back to the initial customer.

Of course, a product like that requires a very important algorithm: given a question about a certain topic, who is the best person in the customer's social network to answer that question? For example, a question about restaurants in San Francisco shouldn't be routed to someone in Seattle. More challenging still, a question about computer programming probably shouldn't be routed to an art student.

Throughout their testing process, Max and Damon encountered many difficult technological problems like these. Each time, they emphatically refused to solve them at that early stage. Instead, they used *Wizard of Oz testing* to fake it. In a Wizard of Oz test, customers believe they are interacting with the actual product, but behind the scenes human beings are doing the work. Like the concierge MVP, this approach is incredibly inefficient. Imagine a service that allowed customers to ask questions of human researchers—for free—and expect a real-time response. Such a service (at scale) would lose money, but it is easy to build on a micro scale. At that scale, it allowed Max and Damon to answer these all-important questions: If we can solve the tough technical problems behind this artificial intelligence product, will people use it? Will their use lead to the creation of a product that has real value?

It was this system that allowed Max and Damon to pivot over and over again, rejecting concepts that seemed promising but that would not have been viable. When they were ready to start scaling, they had a ready-made road map of what to build. The result: Aardvark was acquired for a reported $50 million—by Google.[9]

THE ROLE OF QUALITY AND DESIGN IN AN MVP

One of the most vexing aspects of the minimum viable product is the challenge it poses to traditional notions of quality. The best professionals and craftspersons alike aspire to build quality products; it is a point of pride.

Modern production processes rely on high quality as a way to boost efficiency. They operate using W. Edwards Deming's famous dictum that the customer is the most important part of the production process. This means that we must focus our energies exclusively on producing outcomes that the customer perceives as valuable. Allowing sloppy work into our process inevitably leads to excessive variation. Variation in process yields products of varying quality in the eyes of the customer that at best require rework and at worst lead to a lost customer. Most modern business and engineering philosophies focus on producing high-quality experiences for customers as a primary principle; it is the foundation of Six Sigma, lean manufacturing, design thinking, extreme programming, and the software craftsmanship movement.

These discussions of quality presuppose that the company already knows what attributes of the product the customer will perceive as worthwhile. In a startup, this is a risky assumption to make. Often we are not even sure who the customer is. Thus, for startups, I believe in the following quality principle:

> If we do not know who the customer is, we do not know what quality is.

Even a "low-quality" MVP can act in service of building a great high-quality product. Yes, MVPs sometimes are perceived as low-quality by customers. If so, we should use this as an opportunity to learn what attributes customers care about. This is infinitely better than mere speculation or whiteboard strategizing, because it provides a solid empirical foundation on which to build future products.

Sometimes, however, customers react quite differently. Many famous products were released in a "low-quality" state, and customers loved them. Imagine if Craig Newmark, in the early days of Craigslist, had refused to publish his humble e-mail newsletter because it lacked sufficient high design. What if the founders of Groupon had felt "two pizzas for the price of one" was beneath them?

I have had many similar experiences. In the early days of IMVU, our avatars were locked in one place, unable to move around the screen. The reason? We were building an MVP and had not yet tackled the difficult task of creating the technology that would allow avatars to walk around the virtual environments they inhabit. In the video game industry, the standard is that 3D avatars should move fluidly as they walk, avoid obstacles in their path, and take an intelligent route toward their destination. Famous best-selling games such as Electronic Arts' *The Sims* work on this principle. We didn't want to ship a low-quality version of this feature, so we opted instead to ship with stationary avatars.

Feedback from the customers was very consistent: they wanted the ability to move their avatars around the environment. We took this as bad news because it meant we would have to spend considerable amounts of time and money on a high-quality solution similar to *The Sims*. But before we committed ourselves to that path, we decided to try another MVP. We used a simple hack, which felt almost like cheating. We changed the product so that customers could click where they wanted their avatar to go, and the avatar would teleport there instantly. No walking, no obstacle avoidance. The avatar disappeared and then reappeared an instant later in the new place. We couldn't even afford fancy teleportation graphics or sound effects. We felt lame shipping this feature, but it was all we could afford.

You can imagine our surprise when we started to get positive customer feedback. We never asked about the movement feature directly (we were too embarrassed). But when asked to name the top things about IMVU they liked best, customers consistently listed avatar "teleportation" among the top three (unbelievably, they often specifically described it as "more advanced than *The Sims*"). This inexpensive compromise outperformed many features of the product we were most proud of, features that had taken much more time and money to produce.

Customers don't care how much time something takes to build. They care only if it serves their needs. Our customers preferred the quick teleportation feature because it allowed them to get where they wanted to go as fast as possible. In retrospect, this makes sense. Wouldn't we all like to get wherever we're going in an instant? No lines, no hours on a plane or sitting on the tarmac, no connections, no cabs or subways. Beam me up, Scotty. Our expensive "real-world" approach was beaten handily by a cool fantasy-world feature that cost much less but that our customers preferred.

So which version of the product is low-quality, again?

MVPs require the courage to put one's assumptions to the test. If customers react the way we expect, we can take that as confirmation that our assumptions are correct. If we release a poorly designed product and customers (even early adopters) cannot figure out how to use it, that will confirm our need to invest in superior design. But we must always ask: what if they don't care about design in the same way we do?

Thus, the Lean Startup method is not opposed to building high-quality products, but only in service of the goal of winning over customers. We must be willing to set aside our traditional professional standards to start the process of validated learning as soon as possible. But once again, this does not mean operating in a sloppy or undisciplined way. (This is an important caveat. There is a category of quality problems that have the net effect of slowing down the Build-Measure-Learn feedback loop. Defects make it more difficult to evolve the product. They actually interfere with our ability to learn and so are dangerous to tolerate in any production process. We will consider methods for figuring out when to make investments in preventing these kinds of problems in Part Three.)

As you consider building your own minimum viable product, let this simple rule suffice: remove any feature, process, or effort that does not contribute directly to the learning you seek.

SPEED BUMPS IN BUILDING AN MVP

Building an MVP is not without risks, both real and imagined. Both can derail a startup effort unless they are understood ahead of time. The most common speed bumps are legal issues, fears about competitors, branding risks, and the impact on morale.

For startups that rely on patent protection, there are special challenges with releasing an early product. In some jurisdictions, the window for filing a patent begins when the product is released to the general public, and depending on the way the MVP is structured, releasing it may start this clock. Even if your startup is not in one of those jurisdictions, you may want international patent protection and may wind up having to abide by these more stringent requirements. (In my opinion, issues like this are one of the many ways in which current patent law inhibits innovation and should be remedied as a matter of public policy.)

In many industries, patents are used primarily for defensive purposes, as a deterrent to hold competitors at bay. In such cases, the patent risks of an MVP are minor compared with the learning benefits. However, in industries in which a new scientific breakthrough is at the heart of a company's competitive advantage, these risks need to be balanced more carefully. In all cases, entrepreneurs should seek legal counsel to ensure that they understand the risks fully.

Legal risks may be daunting, but you may be surprised to learn that the most common objection I have heard over the years to building an MVP is fear of competitors—especially large established companies—stealing a startup's ideas. If only it were so easy to have a good idea stolen! Part of the special challenge of being a startup is the near impossibility of having your idea, company, or product be noticed by anyone, let alone a competitor. In fact, I have often given entrepreneurs fearful of this issue the following assignment: take one of your ideas (one of your lesser insights, perhaps), find the name of the relevant product manager at an established company who has responsibility for that area, and try to get that company to steal your idea. Call them up, write them a memo, send them a press release—go ahead, try it. The truth is that most managers in most companies are already overwhelmed with good ideas. Their challenge lies in prioritization and execution, and it is those challenges that give a startup hope of surviving.[10]

If a competitor can outexecute a startup once the idea is known, the startup is doomed anyway. The reason to build a new team to pursue an idea is that you believe you can accelerate through the Build-Measure-Learn feedback loop faster than anyone else can. If that's true, it makes no difference what the competition knows. If it's not true, a startup has much bigger problems, and secrecy won't fix them. Sooner or later, a successful startup will face competition from fast followers. A head start is rarely large enough to matter, and time spent in stealth mode—away from customers—is unlikely to provide a head start. The only way to win is to learn faster than anyone else.

Many startups plan to invest in building a great brand, and an MVP can seem like a dangerous branding risk. Similarly, entrepreneurs in existing organizations often are constrained by the fear of damaging the parent company's established brand. In either of these cases, there is an easy solution: launch the MVP under a different brand name. In addition, a long-term reputation is only at risk when companies engage in vocal launch activities such as PR and building hype. When a product fails to live up to those pronouncements, real long-term damage can happen to a corporate brand. But startups have the advantage of being obscure, having a pathetically small number of customers, and not having much exposure. Rather than lamenting them, use these advantages to experiment under the radar and then do a public marketing launch once the product has proved itself with real customers.[11]

Finally, it helps to prepare for the fact that MVPs often result in bad news. Unlike traditional concept tests or prototypes, they are designed to speak to the full range of business questions, not just design or technical ones, and they often provide a needed dose of reality. In fact, piercing the reality distortion field is quite uncomfortable. Visionaries are especially afraid of a false negative: that customers will reject a flawed MVP that is too small or too limited. It is precisely this attitude that one sees when companies launch fully formed products without prior testing. They simply couldn't bear to test them in anything less than their full splendor. Yet there is wisdom in the visionary's fear. Teams steeped in traditional product development methods are trained to make go/kill decisions on a regular basis. That is the essence of the waterfall or stage-gate development model. If an MVP fails, teams are liable to give up hope and abandon the project altogether. But this is a solvable problem.

FROM THE MVP TO INNOVATION ACCOUNTING

The solution to this dilemma is a commitment to iteration. You have to commit to a locked-in agreement—ahead of time—that no matter what comes of testing the MVP, you will not give up hope. Successful entrepreneurs do not give up at the first sign of trouble, nor do they persevere the plane right into the ground. Instead, they possess a unique combination of perseverance and flexibility. The MVP is just the first step on a journey of learning. Down that road—after many iterations—you may learn that some element of your product or strategy is flawed and decide it is time to make a change, which I call a pivot, to a different method for achieving your vision.

Startups are especially at risk when outside stakeholders and investors (especially corporate CFOs for internal projects) have a crisis of confidence. When the project was authorized or the investment made, the entrepreneur promised that the new product would be world-changing. Customers were supposed to flock to it in record numbers. Why are so few actually doing so?

In traditional management, a manager who promises to deliver something and fails to do so is in trouble. There are only two possible explanations: a failure of execution or a failure to plan appropriately. Both are equally inexcusable. Entrepreneurial managers face a difficult problem: because the plans and projections we make are full of uncertainty, how can we claim success when we inevitably fail to deliver what we promised? Put another way, how does the CFO or VC know that we're failing because we learned something critical and not because we were goofing off or misguided?

The solution to this problem resides at the heart of the Lean Startup model. We all need a disciplined, systematic approach to figuring out if we're making progress and discovering if we're actually achieving validated learning. I call this system innovation accounting, an alternative to traditional accounting designed specifically for startups. It is the subject of Chapter 7.

www.ingramcontent.com/pod-product-compliance
Lightning Source LLC
Chambersburg PA
CBHW060422220526
45465CB00008B/2982